From *Plague* to *Purpose*

From *Plague* to *Purpose*

Sacred Wandering and the Postmodern Church

JOSHUA TAYLOR

WIPF & STOCK · Eugene, Oregon

FROM PLAGUE TO PURPOSE
Sacred Wandering and the Postmodern Church

Copyright © 2022 Joshua Taylor. All rights reserved. Except for brief quotations in critical publications or reviews, no part of this book may be reproduced in any manner without prior written permission from the publisher. Write: Permissions, Wipf and Stock Publishers, 199 W. 8th Ave., Suite 3, Eugene, OR 97401.

Wipf & Stock
An Imprint of Wipf and Stock Publishers
199 W. 8th Ave., Suite 3
Eugene, OR 97401

www.wipfandstock.com

PAPERBACK ISBN: 978-1-6667-5756-9
HARDCOVER ISBN: 978-1-6667-5757-6
EBOOK ISBN: 978-1-6667-5758-3

11/08/22

"The Servant Song" Copyright © 1977 Universal Music—Brentwood Benson Publ. (ASCAP) (admin. at CapitolCMGPublishing.com) All rights reserved. Used by permission.

"We Will Walk With God" Transcribed and Arranged by John L. Bell. Tr. © 2022, arr. © 2008 Wild Goose Resource Group, Iona Community (admin. GIA Publications, Inc.). Used by permission.

"The Summons" by John L. Bell and Graham Maule. Copyright © 1987 Wild Goose Resource Group, Iona Community (admin. GIA Publications, Inc.). Used by permission.

The Holy Bible, English Standard Version® (ESV®) Copyright © 2001 by Crossway, a publishing ministry of Good News Publishers. All rights reserved.

This book is dedicated to Diana. While our paths have since parted ways, her willingness to spend hours listening to me talk about pilgrimage, helping to organize notecards, proofreading, and, most importantly, accompanying me through so many episodes of life, led to the completion of this book. It is also dedicated to my daughters, Hannah and Catherine, who will live with the church that we are shaping through our actions today.

Contents

Acknowledgments		ix
Prologue: My Own Pilgrimage Experience		xi
Introduction: Why Pilgrimage? Why Now?		xvii
1	We Will Walk with God: Pilgrimage, Music, and a Postmodern Church	1
2	O for a Closer Walk with God: Sacred Wandering and Pilgrimage throughout History	20
3	Be My Song as I Journey: The Role of Music on Pilgrimage	37
4	Will You Come and Follow Me?: The Ecumenical Communities of Iona and Taizé—Case Studies of the Modern Pilgrimage	48
5	We'll All Walk Together: Guidelines and Suggestions for Pilgrimage in Local Congregations	66
6	Coda	118
Bibliography		123

Acknowledgments

I am deeply indebted for the guidance Dr. Michael Hawn, Dr. Robert Hunt, and numerous other faculty members of the Perkins School of Theology who inspired and shaped my work throughout the Doctor of Pastoral Music program. This book is the culmination of a journey they encouraged. I would also like to thank my colleagues in the 2017 DPM Cohort who were a constant support. Finally, this book would not be possible were it not for the many opportunities I have had to learn and grow from the congregation members and colleagues at First Presbyterian Church of Dallas, First United Methodist Church of Denton, and the Iona Community. Walking along these saints through the joys and trials of shared ministry has shaped my thoughts on what the postmodern church might look like. These folks give me hope for our shared future.

Prologue

My Own Pilgrimage Experience

The germination of this book began in Dallas, Texas, and it culminated back in Texas, with the road in the middle twisting, turning, running in to dead ends, and hitting unexpected turbulence along the way. Travel has long been important to my own life, and the opportunity to write about the intersection of faith, travel, and music has produced the volume you are holding in your hands or reading on a device. Thanks to the encouragement of my doctoral advisor, this subject served as the topic for my doctoral thesis, which provided the needed impetus to put these words on the page. As the prospectus developed in late 2019, it became clear that God was calling me and my family elsewhere in our life of music ministry. Within weeks of submitting the first draft of my prospectus, my wife Diana and I accepted the position as co-musicians for the Iona Community in Scotland. Writing this book would coincide with our own pilgrimage experience as we moved our two young daughters to a remote island in the Inner Hebrides.

Our journey to Scotland seemed to mimic the tumultuous paths of pilgrims past. As we attempted to sell our home in Texas, leave positions we loved, say our goodbyes, and prepare for an unknown future, we ran into numerous obstacles related to our visa process with the United Kingdom home office. What had been planned for a July arrival on Iona became an October arrival. The sale of our house was also complicated by numerous repairs in the eleventh hour and then extensive damage from a tornado that hit Dallas in late October. A planned sale in early September became

Prologue

November. Parcels were lost, belongings delayed, and, generally speaking, we met disruption and disorientation at each turn. We were definitely pilgrims on a journey.

However, we also met so many people along the way who cared for us, supported us, housed us, fed us, and provided for our journey. In Dallas, friends offered their homes while we were displaced before moving, other friends dropped everything to aid in the repair work when the tornado hit and we were in Scotland, friends in Scotland took us shopping for Iona-appropriate coats, torches (flashlights), and other essentials for surviving a North Sea winter, my mom sent our girls care packages of their favorite candy, and other, non-Iona Community island residents welcomed us into their homes, cooked for us, and invited us into their lives and world. We frequently met Christ in the stranger's guise, and it was Christ who left food in the eating place and drink in the drinking place for us.

Then there was worship and music and lots of time. As someone who has long valued the resources of the Wild Goose Resource Group and the Iona Community, the opportunity to plan worship and music with the community in the abbey church was the impetus for our decision to take the position, uproot our lives, and move to Scotland. We arrived as the tourist season was wrapping up on Iona. The crowds were significantly smaller and everyone who had been there through the hustle and bustle of June, July, and August (when we should have arrived) were looking toward their winter breaks. Additionally, the Iona abbey residence facility was undergoing a major renovation project. Due to this, the Iona Community was severely limited in what programs they could offer. Things were slow. For a worship planner and musician coming from a busy, urban, American congregation, this was an adjustment. Even with worship twice daily at 9:00 a.m. and 9:00 p.m., there was a lot of empty space. After the first month, when the season had officially ended, it became even more empty. Worship crowds went from around 150 on Sunday mornings to ten to fifteen. Morning prayer through the week was down to about eight. This was not unexpected. We had been advised that the winter would be very different than we were used to and a far cry from the experiences I had as

Prologue

a guest on the island in 2016. Still, we pressed on, determined to contribute what we could to the life of the community during this season of transition. Diana learned the guitar, I practiced the piano (a lot) since that was my primary responsibility in the services, we enjoyed the slower pace of school and the extra time with our children, and I wrote— starting this book in the dark days of November and December with the wind howling outside the window.

What we did not realize, at the time, was that our pilgrimage was a healing pilgrimage of sorts. Leaving my previous job in Dallas had been difficult and I was sad. Leaving had been the right choice, but it was challenging, and not making music on a regular basis, working in a sanctuary that I had played a significant role in renovating, or planning worship was devastating. The morning office, with only seven or eight people, was not the same. Yet, the rhythm of worship, different worship, became a gift. "The world belongs to God, **the earth and all its people.** How good it is, how wonderful **to live together in unity.** Love and faith come together, **justice and peace join hands.**" These lines of the Iona morning office became routine, rolling off the tongue as involuntarily as breathing. The simplicity of worship in winter on Iona seemed to be challenging my preconceived notions and expectations of the entire experience.

Christmas was particularly difficult. After years of large Christmas worship services complete with orchestra and choir, combined with busy family schedules, we were in for a very different experience. We were invited to prepare the Christmas Eve choir for the local parish church and spent several weeks working with a small group of singers on simple arrangements of Christmas carols in preparation for the service. On Christmas Eve, we walked to the parish church in the dark (at 5:00 p.m.) and held our candles with maybe fifty people in attendance. We sang "Still the Night" instead of "Silent Night" and "O Little Town of Bethlehem" to FOREST GREEN instead of ST. LOUIS. It was surreal, sad, different, and uplifting, inspiring, and a balm for the soul all at the same time. The experience reaffirmed my call to music ministry in a way that I had not expected. Had I lost my sense of calling? I do not think so, but Iona was affirming that music ministry and my vocation in the church would certainly look different going forward.

Prologue

In January, while home for coursework at SMU, I was approached by a United Methodist Church in Denton, Texas about joining their staff as their Director of Worship and Music, a position very similar to the one I had left in Dallas. It was much sooner than we had expected. Our plan had been to live and work on Iona for three years. After much discussion and prayer, Diana and I decided that the opportunity was too good to pass up. Being back in North Texas, in the town where we had met and married, and closer to family, combined with some ongoing challenges within the Iona Community, seemed like the appropriate move. Our pilgrimage journey was taking another unexpected turn.

As we prepared to return to Texas in the Summer of 2020, the COVID-19 pandemic gripped the world's attention. In mid-March, just a few weeks from Holy Week, the resident staff of the Iona Community attended an all-staff meeting. At the meeting, staff members were advised that it was likely that ferry transportation would soon be restricted. If anyone had plans to leave the island they should go immediately because transportation could not be guaranteed for much longer. Additionally, the community would not be recruiting or filling any staff positions since the lockdown of the United Kingdom meant the construction project would cease, visitors would not be coming, and the community would face a significant financial deficit as a result. The Iona Community would shelter, feed, and pay the staff as long as they could. (On Easter 2020, the Iona Community would launch a new capital appeal to try to sustain their operations.) The same day, the Scottish Government announced that all schools would close at the end of the week indefinitely. After that meeting, held on a Wednesday, we made the hurried plans to leave Iona and Scotland that Saturday. Over the next forty-eight hours, we changed flights, booked train passage and hotel rooms, hastily packed our belongings, and said tearful goodbyes to new friends. Our great adventure, shortened first by choice, was now being brought to a halt by an invisible virus and global pandemic.

Our journey home was one of the most harrowing days of travel we have ever experienced. Shuttered airports shops, deserted planes, and CDC wellness checks were only the beginning of our

Prologue

entrance into an American landscape that was changing in front of our eyes. Our fourteen-day quarantine ended just as most of the state of Texas went under shelter-in-place guidance. We had yet to find a place to live. So, my parents were kind enough to let us stay with them. They even moved into their travel trailer for the fourteen-day quarantine period so that we could be in their home. My new church position allowed me to come on the payroll three months early to help sustain us through the transition. Again, it was the grace, mercy, and generosity of others that sustained us on our pilgrimage.

In the weeks after our arrival back in the United States, I was busy planning worship for the First United Methodist Church in Denton, Texas remotely. Holy Week and Easter were unlike anything I've ever seen. My inclination was to focus on expressions of community in liturgy and song. The resurrected Christ appeared to the disciples in community multiple times. How strange that the best thing we could do in that moment was to be alone, together. Worship services that would have often been elaborate affairs became simplified online gatherings. We held Maundy Thursday worship via Zoom, using a modified version of the Ceildh[1] Communion service from the *Iona Abbey Worship Book*. Perhaps, the simplicity of the Iona experience was exactly the right thing to enter into a church that, out of necessity, had to transform for the moment. Even two years later, I am still not entirely sure. I do know that the space my pilgrimage provided for my life and vocation will never be fully captured in words on a page. Perhaps my perspectives on pilgrimage and the experiences of my own pilgrimage inform the words, thoughts, and ideas in these pages. I hope that is the case. I also sincerely hope that my life has changed as a part of the openness that remote island called forth from me. I cannot point to a specific moment in the abbey church or on the north beach or around the common dinner table as some distinct moment of transformation, but my pilgrimage has changed me, I hope for the better. I hope that it has called me to recognize community at every turn, to value simplicity in worship forms, and to be ready

1. A Ceildh is a traditional Scottish social event that includes dancing, singing, and storytelling.

to change direction quickly. Most importantly, I hope that it helps me to recognize God at work even more acutely than ever before. I believe the COVID-19 pandemic has opened the space for similar changes in our congregations. Perhaps a pilgrimage is what God has in mind for the challenging days of our postpandemic existence. Adopting a pilgrimage approach to our life together in a church that does not look the same is the aim of this book. A dear mentor asked after hearing me describe the precarious nature of things on Iona and then our return, "Do you ever feel like you're not really in control of your life and that some divine force is smiling down on you?" Yes. Every day. May our church communities have the same realization.

Introduction
Why Pilgrimage? Why Now?

INTRODUCTION AND PURPOSE OF THIS STUDY

The reexamination of pilgrimage, along with its relevant music and rituals, has the potential to reshape the liturgical and ecclesiastical structures of the postmodern church. The post-COVID-19 church demands a new way of understanding itself and shaping a new future. The rituals and songs of pilgrimage are some of the ways pilgrims (and pilgrimage groups) construct meaning. They aid in narrating the journey, recounting the stories of those gone before, and in the retelling of the experience upon the pilgrim's return.[2] By studying this discipline, we may discern the ways in which a reengagement with the pilgrimage discipline could impact the modern church's worship practices, music, governance structures, and balance between individual identity and communal existence.

Historically, pilgrimage has had the ability to forge distinctive communities, alter the constructs of meaning for individual pilgrims, and raise awareness of societal structures and tensions. As the practice is being rediscovered in the twenty-first century, any reexamination of pilgrimage must involve more than the geography of the journey. Political, cultural, social, and religious perspectives help to illustrate the role pilgrimage plays in shaping community

---

2. Bohlman, "Final Borderpost," 435.

among pilgrims, local practice, and tradition.³ The music of pilgrimage in particular is embedded in each of these perspectives. By examining the historical foundations of the pilgrimage discipline, the music that has accompanied such journeying, and case studies of modern pilgrimage communities, congregations might be challenged to rethink the static nature of their worship and music and the top-down model of governance pervasive in mainline Protestant churches in America. Undoubtedly, a reexamination of the pilgrimage discipline at the congregational level will require committed collaboration between clergy, musicians, liturgists, lay participants, and other key individuals and may not be accessible in all contexts. The potential disorientation caused by adopting a pilgrimage mindset is explored more fully in the first chapter.

Defining pilgrimage is an elusive and challenging task. The word pilgrimage is derived from the Latin phrase *per agrum*, meaning "through the field," and the noun *peregrinis*, meaning "foreigner, wanderer, exile, traveler, newcomer, or stranger." However, these Latin roots fail to capture the practices, motivations, characteristics, and desired outcomes of the discipline. While rooted in religious origins, the practice of pilgrimage has come to include secular pastimes, activities, and locations, making a broader understanding necessary for current study.⁴ Historical pilgrimage was often focused on healing or the seeking of divine help in a sacred location. Due to this, pilgrimage studies were primarily concerned with the geographical and religious features of these locations. The modern study of pilgrimage, however, has expanded to include discussions of the motivations, shape, dynamics, and effects of pilgrimage on individuals and the communities of which they are a part as well as the journey of life as a metaphorical pilgrimage.⁵ When including these aspects, pilgrimage should also be considered a spiritual discipline as it is a specific intentional action taken to direct individuals (or communities) toward God, with the hope

---

3. Collins-Kreiner, "Researching Pilgrimage," 450.
4. Thomas et al., "To Pray and to Play," 420.
5. Pazos, *Pilgrims and Politics*, 1.

INTRODUCTION

of changing their current practices in the world.[6] For this study, pilgrimage shall be defined as: a spiritual discipline, describing a journey to a sacred center, embarked upon as an act of piety, or an internal journey taken for deeper personal understanding with the hope of transformation.[7] Regardless of its physical or metaphorical nature, the human impulse to embark on pilgrimage has been demonstrated in the Hebrew Scriptures, pilgrimage writings throughout history, and other faith traditions around the world.[8] The traditions and characteristics of this phenomenon, such as simplicity in dress, traveling lightly, and engaging in rituals along the journey, continue to shape individuals and religious communities even today.

The motivations of individuals embarking on pilgrimage are voluntary and diverse.[9] For Christian pilgrims, the motivation may be described as the desire to encounter the risen Lord,[10] while non-Christian pilgrims frequently look to sites of famous architecture, history, books, nature, food, family history, scholars, heroes, and artists for inspiration.[11] Implied is the shared idea that these travelers, regardless of religious affiliation, desire to meet the sacred *in* the world. Thomas Merton poetically describes this search: "There is no program for [seeing God] but the gate of heaven is everywhere."[12] The ways in which these individuals' motivations coalesce through a communal experience and impact the communities from which the pilgrims depart and return continues to have implications for postmodern culture.

While the motivation and definition of a sacred site may differ among pilgrims, a basic structure applies for all such journeys. Dutch anthropologist Arnold van Gennep has described this structure as a rite of passage consisting of three stages: separation,

6. Curran, "Theology as Spiritual Discipline," 3–10.
7. Cousineau, *Art of Pilgrimage*, 25.
8. Collins-Kreiner, "Researching Pilgrimage," 440.
9. Sallnow, "Communitas Reconsidered," 169.
10. Lang, *Pilgrim's Compass*, 26.
11. Cousineau, *Art of Pilgrimage*, 29.
12. Cited in Lang, *Pilgrim's Compass*, 58.

INTRODUCTION

ordeal, and reintegration.[13] This movement is detailed in numerous pilgrimage accounts, perhaps most notably in John Bunyan's *The Pilgrim's Progress*, where Christian, the novel's protagonist, moves from "The Call" and "Departure to Arrival" and "Bringing Back the Boon" in the subsequent chapters of the book.[14] Joseph Campbell's seminal work, *The Hero with a Thousand Faces*, describes this same "monomyth" as the structure undergirding the story of all humanity.[15] Common characteristics of each stage can be recognized in pilgrims' writings from the medieval era to modern times. Openness to the experience, practicing deep attentiveness to surroundings, engaging in spiritual practices (including music), taking gifts, and leaving stories behind mark the stages of the journey.

The departure and initial journey of a pilgrimage is of particular note. This initial journey is often a time of greater freedom and exploration than other phases of pilgrimage. On pilgrimage, which is most often the domain of ordinary people without theological training, the departure begins largely as an individual act outside the hierarchies of organized religion.[16] In departing, the individual pilgrim is separated from their society as well as the structures of their religious institutions, creating tension between the pilgrims' individual motivations and freedom and the rigor and orthodoxy of their local and ecclesial communities.[17] This tension has often had far-reaching implications for secular, religious, and political histories around the world.[18] These historical insights and the ways in which pilgrims change and/or threaten ecclesial power and structure are of primary interest as the discipline of pilgrimage is reclaimed in the twenty-first century. Practically speaking, this portion of the journey frequently includes the exchange of stories, music, gratitude, and gifts between individual pilgrims, their innkeepers, those who feed them, and, perhaps most importantly, their

---

13. Gennep et al., *Rites of Passage*, 10–11.
14. Bunyan, *Pilgrim's Progress*, 1.
15. Campbell, *Hero with a Thousand Faces*, 1–20.
16. Lang, *Pilgrim's Compass*, 4.
17. Socolov, "Pilgrimage," 996.
18. Bohlman, "Final Borderpost," 451.

INTRODUCTION

companions on the road.[19] The experiences of this initial journey have often become the source for creative accounts of pilgrimage, including poetry and music.[20] These accounts provide important insights into the discipline for today's practitioners.

While the departure provides key practices of the journey, the other two movements offer different insights important to the conversation of pilgrimage's potential impact. The arrival at the sacred place is marked by the belief that the divine is close at hand—often described as a thin place. This may also be the site of transformation on pilgrimage. However, reformed understandings of pilgrimage may understand the entire journey as transformative.[21] In reexamining pilgrimage, the moment of transformation is of less importance than the impact the transformation has on the pilgrim's return. In this final stage, the pilgrim returns home, bringing back parts of their experience and a wider worldview which often leaves home as an "elusive destination."[22] While the person of the Latin *peregrinus* longs for home, the pilgrim returns transformed by the stories, music, experience of community, and the ritual of their journey. Anthropologists Victor and Edith Turner focused on this dynamic in their studies of the ritual impacts of pilgrimage. Turner and Turner, writing on pilgrimage as a rite of passage, contended that *communitas*, the intense sense of togetherness, often experienced in ritual experiences where a group stands outside of normal societal structures, had a significant impact on the pilgrim's return to the social structures of "home."[23] The bond between pilgrims has the potential to become more than mere solidarity between travelers, molding into a system of relationship and self-governance with one another.[24] This intense relationship, formed through the

---

19. Cousineau, *Art of Pilgrimage*, 192.

20. Cousineau notes that this period of travel is often met with challenges that have been described by the ancient Greeks as "tests of the gods" and experiences that medieval Japanese travelers believed should become the subjects of poetry and song (43).

21. Robinson, *Sacred Places, Pilgrim Paths*, 2.

22. Lang, *Pilgrim's Compass*, 28.

23. Turner, *Ritual Process*, 94–113.

24. Turner, *Ritual Process*, 132.

INTRODUCTION

pilgrimage experience, has the potential to reshape ecclesial structures upon their return. Chapter 1 will further explore the ways in which pilgrims returning home may bring with them this new structure of *communitas* and be unwilling or unable to return to the established church's ways of understanding. The faith community's response and willingness to adapt to the self-defined, often more speculative and philosophical ideas of *communitas* will determine the success of adopting a pilgrimage mindset for the postmodern church.[25] The definitions of postmodernism are, much like the individual meanings of pilgrimage, varied. For the purposes of this book, postmodernism is defined as a state of being with reactions against established structures, mass consumption, and universal truths. The current decline of the Christian church in the United States suggests that the church has entered a postmodern era. A rediscovery of the pilgrimage discipline may afford the church a way to harmonize its current existence with the less pragmatic and structured views of the pilgrim.[26] With music inseparable from the experiences of pilgrimage, it then also plays a pivotal role in the development of *communitas*, the reshaping of the pilgrim's story, and the potential reforming of societal and ecclesial structures as a result of the discipline.[27] The historical study of pilgrimage, the consideration of its musical components, and a deeper understanding of music's role for modern pilgrimage communities can offer important insights for the ways in which the postmodern church might reclaim the discipline, and its music, for their own benefit in the twenty-first century.

---

25. Turner, *Ritual Process*, 133.
26. Sargeant, *Christian Education and the Emerging Church*, 7.
27. Bohlman, "Final Borderpost," 427.

1

We Will Walk with God

Pilgrimage, Music, and a Postmodern Church

We will walk with God, my brothers; we will walk with God.
We will walk with God, my sisters; we will walk with God.
We will go rejoicing till the kingdom has come.
We will go rejoicing till the kingdom has come.[1]

INDIVIDUALS, PILGRIMAGE, AND PRACTICE

Pilgrimage and its related practices have the ability to change the ecclesiology of the communities touched by the discipline. While individuals embark on pilgrimage for a number of different reasons, their rationale, practice, and definition of the discipline shape their experience, and that of the wider group of which they are a part. This experience reforms their own story as well as the stories of their home communities when they return. The reformed story may potentially change the ecclesiology and worship practices of the faith community. As discussed later in the book, music is integral to the creation of this new story, shaping theological understanding,

---

1. Swaziland text and melody; translated and arranged by John L. Bell, tr. © 2002, arr. © 2008 Wild Goose Resource Group.

mediating the moment of transformation, or becoming a sacred moment in itself. The reexamination of pilgrimage and consideration of the ways in which it might positively shape a new future for the postmodern church must begin with an understanding of the individual.

The reason an individual chooses to embark on pilgrimage may include the desire to pray, to seek metaphorical or literal healing, to gain a blessing, or to gain new perspectives.[2] Because individuals enter the discipline for different reasons, it may be assumed that each will have a unique interpretation of the experience. This suggests that any research on pilgrimage must emphasize subjectivity.[3] This subjectivity must also apply to the music of pilgrimage. That which is sacred, profound, and meaningful for one will not necessarily carry the same meaning for another. This more complex approach suggests that the broad, individual understandings of pilgrimage are relevant to any conversation about the ways the discipline might shape a postmodern church. Focus on definitive sites of pilgrimage or on a specific repertoire of pilgrimage songs would be futile and misses the opportunity to discern the ways in which community is formed through these individual constructs. If a piece of music, a site of pilgrimage, or a specific practice is meaningful to *any* individual on pilgrimage, it is relevant to the community's story.

The pilgrimage discipline, at its heart, is an intentional journey into a liminal experience of unknowing, discomfort, and reorientation for the individual pilgrim. For Christians, the hoped-for transformation of pilgrimage is a new understanding of God that is beyond their original imagination, preconceived expectations, or previous experiences.[4] As the pilgrim is formed by the journey, their worldview, including liturgical and ecclesial expectations, may change. This may require faith communities to expand their liturgical and musical practices to better embrace the diversity of that which the individuals hold as meaningful—a topic explored

---

2. Frank, "Pilgrimage."
3. Collins-Kreiner, "Researching Pilgrimage."
4. Painter, *Soul of a Pilgrim*, 2.

more fully later in this book. Scholar Letty M. Russell calls this "doing theology in a different voice." Russell describes this process as one where traditions are critiqued and reinterpreted through a constructive process focused on community and shared partnership.[5] Whether they embarked on pilgrimage following a significant life event, seeking deeper faith, or for no apparent reason at all, many pilgrims acknowledge that their engagement with the discipline changes their expectations after the journey. The former way cannot return. Faith communities must respond to this new reality.[6]

Pilgrimage is often marked by an intensity and intention for individuals that is difficult to replicate upon their return. However, aspects of the discipline and the continuation of certain practices might reinforce new understandings for individuals and the communities of which they are a part. The belief that the sacred is to be encountered and that movement or journeying is the nexus for such encounter suggests a more fluid approach to liturgical practices, including prayer and music, for both the returned pilgrim and faith communities in the future.[7] Engagement with pilgrimage rituals and traditions suggests that there is something sacred waiting to be discovered in every journey, whether physical or metaphorical. While an encounter may take place in a different location, embracing a pilgrimage mindset at home might lead to a more faithful life for the body of Christ in the community which acknowledges and values the diverse individual's perspectives, values, ways of life, and music.[8]

That which matters to the individual pilgrim should shape the collective understanding of any community of which they are a part. Acceptance of this diverse construct generally requires the faith community to look beyond their current practices and orthodoxy. The faith community may experience their own pilgrimage through this acceptance– a pilgrimage of faith focused on growing discipleship through journeying with the expectation of a

---

5. Russell, *Church in the Round*, 36.
6. Painter, *Soul of a Pilgrim*, 12.
7. Pazos, *Pilgrims and Politics*, 188.
8. Lang, *Pilgrim's Compass*, 64.

holy encounter.[9] History, the biblical narrative, and the continued growth of pilgrimage suggest that this pilgrim spirit already resides in the fabric of faith communities waiting to be embraced by the structures and practice of the church.

The modern understanding of pilgrimage has moved beyond seeing the arrival as its most significant point. The entire journey may be imbued with sacredness. This means that different moments or practices of the journey may become sacramental for individual pilgrims. The individual's ability to absorb meaning at any point of the journey has practical implications for musical and liturgical practices in local congregations. Certain prayers, styles or genres of music, ritual actions, and movements within a worship experience may be more, or less, transformative for an individual. In understanding worship as an extension of pilgrimage practice, worship planners should be highly concerned with that which individuals within their community define as sacred as well as an overarching concern that all music and worship provide space for potential transformation. The reformed worship shaped by pilgrimage becomes a threshold over which individuals cross with the expectation of experiencing something unexpected and transformative.[10] The arrival at this reformed structure may not occur in a logical manner just as individuals do not find meaning on the journey in a calculated way.[11] Rather, the point of pilgrimage, for the individual, is improvement through the rigors and challenge of the journey and, for the postmodern church, is a new reality found through engagement with this community of individual pilgrims.

COMMUNITY, PILGRIMAGE, AND PRACTICE

While it is true that individual pilgrims undertake the discipline for different reasons, pilgrimage does not happen in isolation. Pilgrims are unified in their common direction.[12] Walter Brueggemann sug-

---

9. Lang, *Pilgrim's Compass*, 11.
10. Cousineau, *Art of Pilgrimage*, 123.
11. Cousineau, *Art of Pilgrimage*, 74.
12. George, *Sacred Travels*, 22.

gests that humanness, even in sojourning, is found "in belonging to and referring to that locus in which the peculiar historicity of a community has been expressed and to which recourse is made for purposes of orientation, assurance, and empowerment."[13] In other words, the pilgrim experience is always linked to the history, social constructs, and meaning of *some* community. While historical ideas of family, faith tradition, and culture can no longer be assumed, poststructuralist theories have suggested that meaning is not fixed but rather is shaped in relationship.[14] The Taizé and Iona communities (see chapter 3) demonstrate some ways in which music might be used to shape these relationships and how communal understandings become the dominant feature in pilgrims' postjourneying narrative.

Pilgrims construct the meaning of their journeys together and through experiences with one another.[15] These common experiences may include the sharing of songs, texts, liturgical practices, and other customs from their local communities as well as new rituals created or discovered along the way. In giving up the safety of their own social and ecclesiastical communities, individuals develop bonds with others—often from different social, economic, and faith contexts—while on pilgrimage. The pilgrim, then, is a stranger among strangers, negotiating a new story and practices over the course of their shared journey.

Choosing to enter into this communal experience, Christian pilgrims recognize that Jesus Christ also came as a stranger and, in so doing, questioned political, liturgical, and theological practices along the way. A christological understanding of pilgrimage demands that pilgrims view each interaction with a stranger, new song, practice, or ritual as a potential encounter with the risen Lord.[16] This perspective has ramifications for faith communities as they become increasingly ecumenical and diverse in the twenty-first century and in a post-COVID context.

---

13. Brueggemann, *Land*, 4–5.
14. Rieger, *Faith on the Road*, 71.
15. Bauman, "From Pilgrim to Tourist," 21.
16. Lang, *Pilgrim's Compass*, 63.

As stated, the encounters of pilgrims shape their own individual story as well as their expectations upon their return home. The pilgrimage experience often demands a renewed energy and commitment to an active theology and robust liturgical practices, including music, that challenge social issues and push the bounds of traditional church practice. Joerg Rieger characterizes this new expectation thusly: "Instead of sitting around tables comparing abstract and static theological ideas, [pilgrims] engage in a deeper theological exchange, sharing and comparing actual experiences with the divine and with the theological images they encounter."[17] Congregations wishing to reconcile the experience of individual pilgrims will have to confront the potentially static nature of their buildings, worship orders, music ministries focused on performance, and other deeply held traditions. For pilgrims, the experience of traveling together brings them into solidarity with one another—forcing each individual to give up some control.[18] The same may be necessary for ecclesiastical structures, influenced by pilgrimage, in postmodern society.

The development of *communitas*, the acknowledgment of individual human identity, and a move toward greater universality and unity within the structure of a faith community will require new approaches in liturgical and musical practice. As demonstrated in later chapters, music presents one way to allow space in worship for potential liminal experiences needed to explore these social situations and constructs. Community-based music that requires no prerequisites may allow for the Holy Spirit to work through an experience to create a space in which the community is temporarily equal, having come together for a singular purpose—similar to the pilgrimage experience.[19] However, any radical encounter with "the other"—musical or otherwise—and with a new form of community must not be coercive.[20] The difficult reality facing the postmodern church is that the relationship to the individual pilgrim, their story, and their new reality must be one of connection, expectation, and

---

17. Rieger, *Faith on the Road*, 43.
18. Rieger, *Faith on the Road*, 119.
19. Collins-Kreiner, "Researching Pilgrimage," 449.
20. Rieger, *Faith on the Road*, 110.

hope. The pilgrim will expect that their journeying will also produce a new, meaningful reality for the established community.

Developing mutual relationships among pilgrims, with their individual constructs of meaning, and established patterns of community will take effort. The experiences of Jesus' disciples illustrate the difficulties of leading an antiestablishment life while also suggesting that forming community on the road based on the ideas of pilgrimage comes with its own rewards.[21] Participation in common rituals and music during pilgrimage enhances group cohesion, uniting individual pilgrims into a larger whole.[22] Additionally, pilgrims enter the discipline following in the footsteps of those who have undertaken sacred journeys before them.[23] These realities suggest that the formation of community on pilgrimage and in the local faith community is contextual and relational. Congregations choosing to engage in a wider understanding of the pilgrimage discipline and its implications for their own practice need not think it necessary to change their entire way of being but rather be open to the diverse experiences that individual pilgrims bring to the conversation. Rather, the practice of the community must be dynamic and open to redefinition as they seek to build community to further their ministry.[24]

Just as pilgrims learn songs, rituals, and different theological ideas from fellow travelers and others along their journeys, those who remain at home have something to glean from pilgrim encounters. The impulse to know and love God more fully is a universal trait of the Christian community. The diverse experiences and music of pilgrimage link together this shared quest in a tangible way, and the import of practices, songs, and understandings from the journey enable a wider worldview and reformed story for faith communities. Staying home may provide similar opportunities for growth, but it is their detachment from their communities which allows pilgrims the freedom and space to meet new people, hear new things, and question their assumptions. These realizations

---

21. Rieger, *Faith on the Road*, 34.
22. Kubicki, *Liturgical Music as Ritual Symbol*, 134.
23. Painter, *Soul of a Pilgrim*, 15.
24. Russell, *Church in the Round*, 49.

tangentially broaden the entire community's story.²⁵ When successful, the development of *communitas* as a result of pilgrimage or its practices encourages a broader, deeper, and more inclusive story for society and the church.

FROM NEW STORY TO NEW REALITY

While current research stresses the importance of the individual pilgrim's narrative, it is the wider impact and ramifications of these stories that is most significant for local faith communities.²⁶ The hoped for conclusion of pilgrimage is a new reality. For assemblies embracing pilgrimage ideas, the stories, practices, and energy of the individual pilgrim will shape the wider community's future. The biblical narrative provides an example of this connection. In Philippians 2, Paul admonishes the church at Philippi to acknowledge both their connection to one another as the body of Christ while urging them to resist the temptation to expect individual members to conform to any one person's experience or understanding of faith (Phil 2:4, 14–16). The implication is that each person is to work out their own salvation within the context of the group.²⁷ Adopting a pilgrimage mindset requires the faith community to enact a way of being church that joins people together without negating their individual identities. This way of doing life together requires a new reality for the established faith community.

For these communities, embracing pilgrimage ideals may require the congregation to become strangers within their own practices for the purpose of transformation. This process may not be suitable for all congregations and, as previously stated, will require a collaborative effort between both professional and volunteer participants. Additionally, it may not be necessary for assemblies to enact all aspects of the pilgrimage discipline but rather be open to the way certain elements of a pilgrim's journey are impacting their life together. As with the cycle of pilgrimage for individuals (see

25. Collins-Kreiner, "Researching Pilgrimage," 449.
26. Collins-Kreiner, "Researching Pilgrimage," 448.
27. Lang, *Pilgrim's Compass*, 2.

chapter 2), the faith community may have to embrace disorientation within its common life in order to allow the liminal space necessary to inform this new reality. A focus on the individual narrative and those voices that were marginalized or silenced in the established order during times of social upheaval, technological advances, and greater ecumenicity will push communities to acknowledge their own metaphorical pilgrimage journey. Religion scholar Frederick Ruf suggests that these moments of discomfort are critical to the faith community's transformation. He writes, "What travel means is not just misfortune but seeking misfortune . . . leaving home, stepping into the way that will lead us far away, walking among strangers, being stunned, getting lost—those are religious behaviors."[28] These moments broaden the community's horizons, opening them to features important to the individual pilgrims.

If pilgrimage is to be rediscovered and valued in the postmodern church, the themes, practices, and music that pervade the stories of pilgrims upon their return *should* also shape the reality of the communities of which they are a part. Pilgrims' stories, rituals, songs, and other types of content suggest what holds meaning for the diverse pilgrimage population.[29] For faith communities, embracing this content in the contexts of church governance, liturgical, and musical practices will likely cause discomfort. However, it may be this reformation of church practices that becomes the catalyst for a renewed life together. The pilgrim's individual story, brought back from their journey, is the final part of the pilgrimage experience, and a community's failure to accept it or incorporate it into their own way of being potentially negates the possible benefits of the discipline and represents the maintenance of the status quo.

The potential benefits of pilgrimage for the postmodern church are only realized when the faith community acknowledges that choosing to walk with the pilgrim will create work and challenge for their community. Incorporating the practices of pilgrims into the church's life demands that the church look critically at its music, liturgy, governance, education, and way of relating to one

---

28. Ruf, *Bewildered Travel*, 4.
29. Thomas et al., "To Pray and to Play," 412.

another to include that which holds meaning for each individual. This incorporation must reach beyond an oversentimentalized, romantic, or exotic view of pilgrimage to one of deep contemplation and commitment to understanding the discipline's benefits to the local assembly. Musically, it is likely that understanding pilgrimage will require the songs of the church to stretch beyond the dichotomies of traditional versus contemporary, Western and non-Western musical idioms, and, potentially, beyond the realms of sacred and secular. Similar considerations are also necessary in relation to visual arts, architecture, governance, and language, among others. In short, embracing pilgrimage practices and ideals will inevitably push the faith community beyond their normal comfort zones.

The departure from the status quo is a regular feature for pilgrimage journeys.[30] The characteristic simplicity of pilgrims' journeying suggests that living and operating in an alternative way creates meaning and value. However, the pilgrim's journey is also marked by uncertainty and a general lack of control. In choosing to embark on pilgrimage, pilgrims give up their social, political, and ecclesial moorings in hope of transformation. This reality of the discipline suggests jarring consequences for communities embracing it. As Dietrich Bonhoeffer points out, however, "if we truly want to find God, we have to look for God where God has preceded us."[31] As will be discussed in chapter 2, journeying and pilgrimage ideas are fundamental to the biblical narrative. With this in mind, embracing such practices may become a way of rediscovering identity as much as changing it. It is important to remember that the current pilgrim's experience is also connected to the experience of previous pilgrims, rooting any transformation in a shared historical narrative. Giving up control in polity, liturgy, and music in the name of more widely embracing individual constructs allows space for the work of the Holy Spirit to create meaning beyond the church's efforts to define God only through their previous understandings.[32]

---

30. Rieger, *Faith on the Road*, 65.
31. Bethge, *Dietrich Bonhoeffer*, 771.
32. Lang, *Pilgrim's Compass*, 73–74.

Just as the pilgrimage community finds liminal space in shared rituals, churches may also discover a new reality through the examination of their current practice and an openness or rediscovery of different rituals which unite individuals.[33] Music has the potential to play a significant role in this discernment. Attention to, and a wider embrace of, diverse musical practices encourages the formation of community when *everyone's* song is included. Acknowledgment and naming of this practice brings an awareness to a new way of being as a result of pilgrimage. This inclusion brings the recollection of the individual pilgrim into the shared practice of the faith community in a meaningful way and allows their definitions of what is sacred to permeate the collective conscience of the entire group.

The substance and practicalities of embracing these pilgrimage ideals, however, reaches beyond fluidity of form. As demonstrated in historical writings, engagement in pilgrimage had far-reaching political, social, and theological impacts. This suggests that the new story of the individual pilgrim also contains reformed ideas, subject matter, and expectations. What has been traditionally considered sacred may be rediscovered or discarded. The liminal space of pilgrimage has the potential to create new awareness of, relationship with, and sacredness around people and issues that challenge traditional hierarchies.[34] Victor W. Turner's research pointed to pilgrimage as a disruptor of processual units and societal structure. This insight suggests that the music of pilgrimage and its other practices may reach well beyond simple stylistic changes to fundamentally changing a community's identity.[35] On a larger scale, pilgrimage treaties, negotiations with political leaders, and the discipline's ability to transcend national and religious borders seem to indicate its ability to change whole societies.[36] Regardless of scale, a deeper understanding of pilgrimage will require faith communities

---

33. Pazos, *Pilgrims and Politics*, 187.
34. Rieger, *Faith on the Road*, 67.
35. Kubicki, *Liturgical Music as Ritual Symbol*, 134.
36. Stokes, "Travel and Tourism," 150.

to examine the content of their worship and music in relationship to how it lines up with the pilgrim's desired societal outcome.

As pilgrimage continues to expand with greater globalization, different ways of understanding society and shaping it through music, worship, and church structures will be required for the faith community to remain relevant. Pastor Paul Lang connects this reality to Christ's teaching on the greatest commandment, "Love God with all [your] heart . . . and love [your] neighbor as yourself. Not a one of the elements of this imperative requires the participation of the neighbor."[37] In pilgrimage, the boundaries of society, faith, and inclusion of diverse individuals with different constructs of meaning are broken down. The new story and new reality as a result of pilgrimage require the faith community to reach beyond itself, opening itself to a wider worldview through which the pilgrim may pass.[38]

It is difficult to define the specific ways in which the church may need to stretch and dissolve these boundaries. Conceiving of alternative forms of structure will be uniquely contextual for each congregation but most certainly will vary from the current status quo. The connection to "heaven on earth" described by pilgrims demands an alternative physical world different from their previous situation.[39] Examining the experiences of pilgrims, however, does provide some insight.

The development of *communitas* among pilgrims is frequently described as the liminal moment when class distinctions fall away in favor of homogeneity among the pilgrimage community.[40] This connects the embrace of pilgrimage ideals with justice. For faith communities, embracing the pilgrimage discipline requires interacting with, valuing, and incorporating the stories, traditions, music, and perspectives of those beyond their walls, creating what Turner calls a "flowing process" between the various groups.[41]

---

37. Lang, *Pilgrim's Compass*, 1.
38. Bohlman, "Final Borderpost," 440.
39. Rieger, *Faith on the Road*, 65.
40. Kubicki, *Liturgical Music as Ritual Symbol*, 133.
41. Turner, "Passages, Margins, and Poverty," 398.

Moving beyond the status quo has the potential to powerfully reshape the community and, for Christian pilgrims and faith communities, to acknowledge God's role in shaping the community beyond their own control.

Already, the greater opportunities for American travelers to be exposed to differing voices in the world church have shaped liturgical and musical practices in the church—as evidenced in the incorporation of Taizé and Iona music in mainline, Protestant hymnals. The wider inclusion of global song and music from varying denominational and racial backgrounds suggests that traveling and individual stories or songs have become part of the church's regular practice. However, other communities remain underrepresented or excluded.[42] Adopting a pilgrimage approach calls for the inclusion of these perspectives. Rieger suggests that venturing further "off the path" may result in a "hybridity—the fused nature of identity that welds together [the] dominant and repressed" in one person or community.[43] It bears repeating that this phenomenon requires the active incorporation of minority voices and perspectives as well as the relinquishment of control by the dominant community.[44]

As was often the case for the communities through which pilgrims traveled, change, as a result of pilgrims' experiences, is inevitable. With the ease of contemporary travel and access to musical, liturgical, and spiritual resources via the internet, these narratives and practices are already informing the contexts of meaning for individual congregation members. For faith communities, these constructs may vary radically from the ideas and concepts of the (currently) dominant church.[45] The ways in which churches are able

---

42. A Pew Research Center study ("Global Christianity") shows that as the world population grows the center of Christianity (and its growth) has shifted to the Global South, and yet worship forms and music still remain highly European/American-centric. The ways in which pilgrimage to these new locations of the faith, their practices, and their music may shape the American church remains to be seen.

43. Rieger, *Faith on the Road*, 68.

44. Sandra Maria van Opstal explores this hybridity in the construction of worship teams in her book, *The Next Worship: Glorifying God in a Diverse World*.

45. Rieger, *Faith on the Road*, 19.

to adopt and incorporate these ideas, stretching beyond their current status quo, may shape their relevancy in a postmodern society. Pilgrimage suggests that churches must adopt a new understanding of themselves not as builders of the kingdom but as sojourners in search of the city "who's designer and builder is God" (Heb 11:10 ESV). Pilgrimage does not negate the previous world of the faith community but rather adapts it, creating an alternative construct of that world.

NEW OUTLOOKS FOR A NEW CHURCH

As the American church continues to change in the twenty-first century and following the COVID-19 pandemic, different approaches, understandings, and practices will be necessary for its continued relevance and survival. With declining attendance numbers, less traditional and more individualistic practices such as pilgrimage may become necessary guideposts for the established faith community's future.[46] Postmodernity has shown that individuals are choosing to belong to fewer organized communities.[47] The church's ability to adapt, adjust, and incorporate pilgrims' individual religious identities in their structures and practice is significant for its future life.

Incorporating these individual identities, including music, prayer, and rituals, alongside traditional structures and orthodoxy will take time, study, and intentional actions. The established congregation must work to find a balance between individual experiences of transformation and empowering a sustainable, workable community of individuals.[48] This will likely result in churches reconsidering the location, times, substance, and results of their programming, including the music ministry, worship experiences, meetings, and other aspects of their community. While membership in the church community was once defined by individual members fitting into these predefined structures, postmodernity and the

---

46. Thomas et al., "To Pray and to Play," 412.
47. Rieger, *Faith on the Road*, 72.
48. Lang, *Pilgrim's Compass*, 3.

adoption of a pilgrimage mindset requires churches to consider the pilgrim first. The pilgrim plays a significant role in the definition of what is sacred for the community, challenging the homeostasis of the established organization.

For the church embracing a pilgrimage mindset, this challenge to their authority and structure is not unexpected. Movement away from a static theology and way of being is embedded within the pilgrimage discipline. Movement away from certitudes toward a more flexible understanding of approach and community is essential for the pilgrimage church. Brother Roger's commitment to living in the provisional at Taizé provides one important example of this mindset. The prayers, worship experiences, times, locations, rehearsals, and outcomes must be amendable in the name of the individual developing a closer relationship with God. Movement is at the heart of this approach—regardless of physical movement or not. Pilgrimage requires the church community to be light on its feet and ready for change.

The change of a pilgrimage church is really more a perpetual time of transition.[49] Informed by the past, looking toward the future, but rooted in the present, *communitas* is developed within these communities by their shared commitment to, and respect for, connection with one another and authenticity within their shared experience.[50] This perpetual transition represents the community's own metaphorical pilgrimage—a journey that faith communities often fail to acknowledge. Evaluation of local traditions and a turn from a "that's the way we always do it" mentality may incorporate more pilgrimage practice into the local community's existence.

Additionally, the commitment to individual development and a shared collective meaning requires the established faith community to adapt to different individuals' perspectives. Archbishop Desmond Tutu describes this type of community as a place of *ubuntu* that is, "a place of community, where every single person matters and where no one is diminished since that would lead to

---

49. George, *Sacred Travels*, 16.
50. Thomas et al., "To Pray and to Play," 412.

the diminishment of all."[51] This does not mean that conflict is removed from the church experience but rather that it is suspended for the purposes of *communitas*.[52]

For the pilgrimage church, former understandings of their life together are not erased but rather the community is one of compromise and adaptation. M. J. Sallnow defines this relationship as one where "differences are accepted or tolerated rather than aggravated into grounds of aggressive opposition."[53] Again, music may provide the best opportunity for dialogue around these understandings. Similar to the ways in which the Iona Community has used new hymn texts to speak of sensitive and often divisive social issues (discussed more fully in chapter 3), the music of the church may provide an opportunity to open a dialogue about challenges between the church's orthodoxy and the individual pilgrim's context of meaning and social outlook. In adopting pilgrimage attributes, it is necessary to never lose connection with the individual.

Discipleship, by its nature, is always an individual act. Similar to pilgrimage, discipleship may happen in the context of a community and be shaped by that community's structures, compromises, and identity, but it remains an individual undertaking.[54] The postmodern church's ability to harness this individuality for their own success is dependent upon acknowledging this reality. Organizational narcissism is the opposite of the pilgrimage mindset. The transformation of pilgrimage happens when the individual pilgrim departs from their existing communities, embracing a new, radically changed reality; the same may be true for faith communities.

Reflecting on the experience of the pilgrim may encourage organizations to consider what practices and adaptations to their life together might produce their own liminal moments. Allowing space for a sense of liminality to pervade their spiritual and organizational understandings also invites a wider conversation

---

51. Santos, *Community Called Taizé*, 9.
52. Thomas et al., "To Pray and to Play," 413.
53. Sallnow, "Communitas Reconsidered," 164.
54. Lang, *Pilgrim's Compass*, 8.

about what is happening within their community.[55] For Christian churches, this liminality also produces a deeper understanding and recognition that God is at work not just in their community but in communities around the world. The dissemination of Taizé music around the world demonstrates how global practices may inform local practice when congregations open themselves to the experiences of pilgrimage.[56] Of course, this openness comes with risks and potential failure for the faith community. Acknowledgment that the world around them is changing, seeking a deeper understanding of pilgrimage ideas, will require resiliency.

The recognition that maintenance of the status quo is no longer an option is critical for faith communities considering the pilgrimage discipline as insight for a different future. Just as the pilgrim is at home in their sojourning, the pilgrimage church must recognize that incorporation of individual constructs of meaning, shaped within community, for the purposes of transformation, *is* a critique of current practice. Additionally, the acknowledgment that this critique and adjustment comes with no guarantee will require humility from all involved. Mistakes, challenges, and failures are an inevitable part of the pilgrim's journey.[57] Regardless, the rediscovery of the pilgrimage discipline for a postmodern church requires the church to embrace an active theology embodied in an active discernment of individual meaning, common practices (including prayer and music), and a willingness to move beyond the status quo.

POSTMODERN CONSIDERATIONS

In the postmodern era, pilgrimage affords the established faith community the opportunity to embrace individuals in their own quests for meaning while building authentic community through shared experiences, rituals, and music. This requires evaluation of their existing practices and a commitment to adopting a theology inspired by movement and sojourning. This theology is not new

---

55. Power, "Place of Community," 34.
56. Kubicki, "Pilgrimage."
57. Painter, *Soul of a Pilgrim*, 19.

and is rooted in the historical and authentic past of the biblical narrative and previous pilgrims (see chapter 2). The acknowledgment of this connection between pilgrimage's past, present, and future is essential for the complete realization of the discipline's ideals.[58] The quest for meaning and truth is one that reaches beyond time and tradition. Current pilgrimage joins this already rich story while accepting an unknown future.

A pilgrim's or pilgrimage community's acceptance of something different than their status quo is necessary for growth. As Phil Cousineau notes, "patience, silence, trust, and faith are venerable qualities of the pilgrim, but more important is the *practice* of them."[59] Pilgrimage, its practices, music, and rituals may expand the horizons of an individual or community's faith and provide greater understanding of their lifelong spiritual journey, but it is likely to be gained through challenges to their previous existence. This alone may make the adoption and enactment of pilgrimage difficult for established faith communities. The imagination of the pilgrim is best captured when communities are able to move through this anxiety to an unknown sacred moment awaiting.

The discovery of the sacred through pilgrimage will inevitably require a time of provisional and transitional approach to liturgical, theological, physical, and musical practices in the church.[60] This way will likely be fraught with mistakes, changes, and discomfort. The simplicity of the pilgrimage discipline suggests that its success hinges on the ability to find peace and humility in these moments.[61] Dean MacCannell, a sociologist, offers this reflection about pilgrimage's humility and room for error:

> The true heroes are those who leave home not knowing where they will end up, never knowing whether their eventual end will connect meaningfully to their origins, knowing only that their future will be made of dialogue

---

58. Thomas et al., "To Pray and to Play," 413.
59. Cousineau, *Art of Pilgrimage*, 172 (emphasis original).
60. Lang, *Pilgrim's Compass*, 28.
61. Cousineau, *Art of Pilgrimage*, 130.

with their fellow travelers and those they meet along the way.[62]

Pilgrimage, for the faith community, will be about learning as they go and rediscovering themselves along the way.

The next chapter will explore the historical and biblical foundations of this ancient discipline, providing insights into the ways in which pilgrimage has been and already is a part of the postmodern church's identity.

---

62. MacCannell, *Empty Meeting Grounds*, 4–5.

2

O for a Closer Walk With God
Sacred Wandering and Pilgrimage throughout History

O for a closer walk with God,
a calm and heav'nly frame,
a light to shine upon the road
that leads me to the Lamb!

So shall my walk be close with God,
calm and serene my frame;
so purer light shall mark the road
that leads me to the Lamb.[1]

SACRED WANDERING IN THE BIBLICAL WITNESS

While pilgrimage is practiced by many faith traditions, the Hebrew Scriptures and the Christian New Testament provide specific examples of the discipline as a significant ritual in a life of faith. The

---

1. William Cowper (1772), "O for a Closer Walk with God." See: https://hymnary.org/text/o_for_a_closer_walk_with_god.

lives of many individuals throughout both testaments are shaped and transformed through their respective journeys. Accounts of Abraham (née Abram), the exodus, and the visit of the magi offer evidence of the contribution of sacred travel in the development of both Judaism and Christianity.[2] The Hebrew word for pilgrim, *magor,* is an odd modification of the word for "dwelling" or "home," but slightly changed to mean "place of sojourning."[3] The tension between home and the practice of sojourning provides the setting for understanding the lives of Abraham, Moses, Paul, and even Jesus Christ as people whose lives were transformed and defined in their journeying.

For Christians, encountering God in Scripture means encountering a pilgrim God who tells God's stories through the lives of other pilgrims. The Pentateuch provides numerous accounts of those whom God has called being shaped through pilgrimage. Adam and Eve are sent from the garden. Cain wanders east of Eden. Abram and Sarai respond to God's call to depart Haran to spend the majority of their lives wandering.[4] Moses participates in several sacred journeys: leaving Egypt for Sinai, returning to Egypt, and, finally, leading the exodus of the Israelites in search of the promised land. God's call to Abram provides a clear biblical basis for pilgrimage in Genesis 12:1–2 (ESV): "Go from your country and your kindred and your father's house to the land that I will show you. I will make of you a great nation, and I will bless you, and make your name great, so that you will be a blessing." Theologian Joerg Rieger understands this journey as the model for what God expects of God's people in the future: "Consider how much of the material of Jewish and Christian traditions actually developed on the road. There is nothing static about Abraham, regarded as one of the pillars of the faith."[5] His journey, and the journeys of other biblical characters, becomes the impetus for learning theological lessons. In the case of the exodus or the period of Babylonian exile,

---

2. George, *Sacred Travels,* 17.
3. Lang, *Pilgrim's Compass,* 19.
4. Lang, *Pilgrim's Compass,* 10–11.
5. Rieger, *Faith on the Road,* 17.

the Israelites develop significant understandings about God and their relationship with God. These early pilgrimages were also accompanied by song, as evidenced in the songs of Miriam and Moses at the Red Sea (Exod 15), the song of wells in the wilderness (Num 21), Joshua, and the psalms of the exile among others. The journeys of Old Testament characters also mirror the circular motion of pilgrimage with the departure, the journey—including challenges, failures, sufferings—and the return to a transformed "home."[6] In all instances, these journeys are foundational to the community's religious identity.

The Gospel narratives about the life of Jesus of Nazareth echo this pattern. In Matthew's account of Christ's incarnation, Mary and Joseph are forced to travel to Bethlehem and then flee to Egypt before returning to Galilee (Matt 2; Luke 2). Emmanuel—God with Us (Matt 1:23)—describes God making God's own pilgrimage, leaving God's "home" in order to sojourn with humanity.[7] Christ's journey to Calvary (Matt 27:31–33; Mark 15:20–22; Luke 23:26–32; John 19:16–18) is particularly significant as subsequent Christian pilgrimages have identified and followed the footsteps of Christ's final journey to the cross.[8]

Journeying is also a distinguishing characteristic of those who follow Jesus in the New Testament. Jesus seems to be very concerned that the faith development of those who do not travel and choose to stay in their homes and communities will be significantly compromised.[9] He provides instruction for how pilgrims should be welcomed on the road in Hebrews 13:2: "Do not neglect to show hospitality to strangers," and in Matthew 25:35: "I was a stranger and you welcomed me," as well as instructions for how to travel, "[take] no bag for your journey; or two tunics" (Matt 10). The New Testament provides insights and instruction into the practice for those called "people of the Way" in the book of Acts, and the lives of Paul, Peter, and James (among others) mirror a life of pilgrimage.

---

6. Rieger, *Faith on the Road*, 29.
7. Lang, *Pilgrim's Compass*, 11–12.
8. Robinson, *Sacred Places, Pilgrim Paths*, 2.
9. Rieger, *Faith on the Road*, 34.

The title, "people of the Way," implies a life of movement in response to Jesus' call to "follow me."[10]

Early Christians, drawing on biblical examples, maintained the practices of these scriptural journeys and developed their own *christologia viatorum* (Christology of travelers and pilgrims) and other theological insights through sacred travel.[11] The transitory nature of the early church was rooted in the expectation of an "age to come" and recalls that Jesus' life and ministry was pervaded throughout by a sense of movement.[12] As a result, pilgrimage routes and practices became an essential element in religious formation.

The connection between God's own pilgrimage and the pilgrimage of God's people and music might best be illustrated in the book of Psalms. The Psalms of Ascent (literally, songs of the steps) are widely considered by biblical scholars to refer to pilgrimage.[13] As reflected in the title, "songs" suggests that these psalms (120–34) are not just to be read but are to be sung and enacted along the pilgrimage route. Pastor and Psalms scholar Melinda Cousins holds that: "The Psalms invite us into an experience of conversing with God, and with one another about God, and it is from this conversational experience that our theology is shaped."[14] In all pilgrimages, it is these conversations that lead to relationships and the development of *communitas* among pilgrims. The Psalms of Ascent and the biblical narratives provide key perspectives of pilgrimage's impact on the early church and ways in which it might still shape the church today.

MEDIEVAL AND EARLY PILGRIMAGE

Sites associated with the biblical narrative became the earliest destinations for sacred travels in the opening centuries of the Christian church. This mirrored Jewish tradition which had included

10. Rieger, *Faith on the Road*, 15.
11. Rieger, *Faith on the Road*, 39.
12. K. M. George, cited in Robinson, *Sacred Places, Pilgrim Paths*, 14–15.
13. Cousins, "Conversing," 37.
14. Cousins, "Conversing," 35.

pilgrimage festivals (Passover, Pentecost, and Tabernacle) that drew large crowds to Jerusalem until the temple's destruction in 70 CE.[15] Following the legalization of Christianity by Constantine in 312 CE, Constantine's mother began promoting travel to Jerusalem and other sites associated with Jesus Christ as an act of discipleship.[16] Faith formation for early Christians relied on individual transformation embodied through prayer (both corporate and private), silence, and solitude, with pilgrimage becoming a way to live a faithful life in the time before Christianity became a nearly exclusive intellectual pursuit.[17] Medieval pilgrims, like their modern-day counterparts, embarked on this enacted response of faith for different reasons, with individuals citing prayer, healing, guidance, intercessions, oracles, or penance as the impetus for their departure.[18] These early travelers to the Holy Land embraced storytelling as an important aspect of their journey, leaving behind a number of important writings describing their journeys.[19] While much of the scholarship around these early pilgrimages has primarily focused on the significance of the physical sites, these writings provide insights into the practices of pilgrims that remain applicable for current considerations of the discipline.

Historical records of pilgrimage exist from the second century onwards. The earliest recorded Christian pilgrimage was in 170 CE by Milito of Sardis to Jerusalem,[20] with the peak of Christian pilgrimage occurring during the twelfth and thirteenth centuries when it was considered a "major investment in eternal life."[21] Providing one of the most complete accounts of early pilgrimage was a pilgrim from Gaul, likely named Egeria, who wrote extensively of her travels to Egypt, Palestine, Syria, and Asia Minor during the late fourth century. The Spanish nun's journal provides insight into

15. Frank, "Pilgrimage," 826.
16. Frank, "Pilgrimage," 827.
17. Lang, *Pilgrim's Compass*, 7.
18. Sallnow, "Communitas Reconsidered," 169.
19. Interestingly, many of these early writings are by and about female pilgrims.
20. Robinson, *Sacred Places, Pilgrim Paths*, 3.
21. Rieger, *Faith on the Road*, 64.

the early practices of Christian pilgrims. Egeria notes at which sites she received a *eulogia* (a blessing or sacred object) from her hosts, which usually consisted of local fruit or, occasionally, a copy of a sacred text.[22] Her writing, as well as other accounts, point to simplicity as an overarching philosophy of these early pilgrims. They describe how travelers carried only a single satchel and provide details on the simplicity of dress and diet necessary for pilgrims negotiating the physical requirements of their journeys.[23]

As pilgrimage grew in popularity, the large influx of travelers required infrastructure to support them along the road, including inns, hostels, roads, and protection, as well as vendors selling food, clothing, and souvenirs. The hospitals became important places of welcome and hospitality for strangers—offered to those who lacked resources (or those who refused to share their resources)—and significant places of interaction between pilgrims and the communities through which they traveled.[24] Sacred traveling created tension between these different communities, leading social and ecclesial authorities to attempt regulating travelers' behavior, albeit with limited success. Within the church, Christian writers offered differing opinions of pilgrimage. The theologian Jerome (347–420 CE) mostly supported pilgrimage efforts and encouraged many to follow the lead of the "blessed Paula," an early pilgrim, in traveling to, and even settling permanently in, the Holy Land.[25] Augustine of Hippo (354–430 CE) described Christian discipleship as a metaphorical pilgrimage, but not all writers looked favorably on the practice.[26] Gregory of Nyssa (335–94 CE) recognized the transformational possibilities of pilgrimage but warned that women needed to return to the "routine of ascetic life in the home."[27] He feared that seeking God in a distant place confined God to that place. Athanasius of Alexandria discouraged monks from pursuing pilgrimage,

---

22. Frank, "Pilgrimage," 827.
23. Socolov, "Pilgrimage," 997.
24. Pazos, *Pilgrims and Politics*, 124.
25. F. E. Peters, cited in Robinson, *Sacred Places, Pilgrim Paths*, 14.
26. Lang, *Pilgrim's Compass*, 12.
27. Gregory of Nyssa, *On the Soul and the Resurrection*, 30–31.

fearing that it compromised the separation of the sexes.[28] These negative opinions were eventually codified at the Council of Chalcedon (451 CE) which imposed strict limits on monastic travels.[29] These warnings and the edicts of the council seem to have had little success. Regarding wandering, St. Francis of Assisi (1182–1226) wrote: "I encouraged the brothers in obedience to have no place of their own, neither house nor any other thing; but they shall be as strangers and pilgrims and servants of God in this world."[30] His writings and the continued practice of pilgrimage suggests that, if pilgrimage had a downside, it was not apparent from the pilgrims' personal accounts.[31] Pilgrimage, in its earliest forms, was outside of the church's normal orthodoxy. Today, it often remains beyond the norms of ecclesial structure and frequently challenges the church's authority and the wider political and social landscapes.

THE POLITICS OF PILGRIMAGE

Since its earliest history, pilgrimage has shaped the political and civil discourses of communities associated with the pilgrims' departure, travel, and return. Early pilgrims risked their communal, civic, and economic existence when engaging in the pilgrimage discipline.[32] Additionally, pilgrimage is shown to have influenced global trade and health.[33] Just as the early church was impacted by these journeys, the political structures of communities were also touched, and in some instances changed, by these travelers. Christian, Muslim, and Jewish pilgrims have, throughout history, been forced to negotiate changing political landscapes, particularly in the Latin East, resulting in political protections, treaties, and safe passage laws for pilgrims around the world.[34] In an early example

28. Frank, "Pilgrimage," 830.
29. Frank, "Pilgrimage," 831.
30. Cited in Robinson, *Sacred Places, Pilgrim Paths*, 16–17.
31. Frank, "Pilgrimage," 830.
32. Rieger, *Faith on the Road*, 64.
33. Collins-Kreiner, "Researching Pilgrimage," 441.
34. Pazos, *Pilgrims and Politics*, 4.

of such political negotiations, Francis of Assisi negotiated rights for Christian worshipers (and the Franciscan order) to have a presence in the sacred sites of Jerusalem during the Muslim rule of al-Nâsir Muhammad, Mamluk sultan of Egypt in 1333, which began a compromise over territory in the holy city that continues today.[35] It is important to consider pilgrimage's ability to shape similar political realities through its practice today.

The intersection of politics and pilgrimage has been, and continues to be, particularly acute in Rome. Rome functions as both a site of pilgrimage and the center of business and administrative activities for the pope and his cardinals in the Curia, the administrative heart of the papacy.[36] This link sets the connection between the practice of pilgrimage and the political activities of ecclesial leaders at center stage. Historically, the established church resented the movement and re-creation of life by pilgrims, as evidenced in the Council of Chalcedon's efforts, but pilgrimage to Rome met the church's need to try to control pilgrims even while tacitly allowing their journeying. In Rome, the reconciliation of individual pilgrims' needs and individual constructs with the church's corporate, institutional existence is paramount to understanding the ways in which the reexamination of this discipline in the twenty-first century might allow modern-day churches to achieve a similar balance.

Beyond Rome, medieval rulers frequently used pilgrimage routes and the pilgrims themselves to support their own political ambitions. Pilgrimage was used as the basis for the First Crusade and, into the fifteenth century, as a pawn in political negotiations.[37] English kings frequently used images of pilgrimage to describe their political movements—invoking divine aid for wars by visiting shrines prior to battle. As Robert N. Swanson notes: "[For English kings] there was always a political element to their spirituality, and a spiritual element to their politics."[38] This coercive use of pilgrimage suggests that acknowledging pilgrimage, accommodating pilgrims,

---

35. Tolan, *Saint Francis and the Sultan*, 258.
36. Pazos, *Pilgrims and Politics*, 92.
37. Pazos, *Pilgrims and Politics*, 55.
38. Cited in Pazos, *Pilgrims and Politics*, 30.

and providing for their safety have proved to be in the political, economic, and ideological interests of rulers throughout the world. It also suggests that pilgrims have their own political power.

While early pilgrims gave up the security of their own communities, in so doing they were able to construct new ways of life for themselves. This reality dramatically impacted the communities of which they were a part. The ecclesiastical and theological critiques of pilgrimage might be reread as a criticism of the pilgrims' desire for autonomy and freedom of experience.[39] Additionally, their interactions with one another shaped human interactions over greater distances, resulting in a new community formed apart from, and at times in opposition to, traditional civic and church structures.[40] This connection between pilgrims and new community development leads to the question of how pilgrimage might continue to shape civil structure in a postmodern context.

PILGRIMAGE AS INSPIRATION

The stories and experiences of these early pilgrims continued to offer meaning for future pilgrims beyond the medieval era. Early pilgrimages focused on broad themes that have remained relevant to travelers and shaped post-Reformation thought around the discipline, including: the lived connections of sacred travel, the unexpected encounters, the visual content, and the quest for personal transformation.[41] Many of the Reformers including Martin Luther (1483–1546), John Calvin (1509–64), William Tyndale (1494–1536), Thomas More (1478–1535), and Thomas Cranmer (1489–1556) wrote of discipleship as a metaphorical pilgrimage.[42] Pilgrimage remained a pervasive idea even as society and the church changed dramatically. While the Reformers did not endorse physical pilgrimage, their references show the powerful

---

39. Frank, "Pilgrimage," 830.
40. Cited in Pazos, *Pilgrims and Politics*, 124.
41. Thomas et al., "To Pray and to Play," 412.
42. Lang, *Pilgrim's Compass*, 13.

imagery it provided for describing life, faith, and the search for enlightenment.[43]

Figure 1: Flammarion, *Pilgrim Astronomer*, Public Domain

Even as theologians spoke only metaphorically about pilgrimage, the practice continued and served as a source of inspiration for laypersons and nontheological writers into the twentieth century. Among others, Geoffrey Chaucer's (1343–1400) *Canterbury Tales* provides one of the most significant literary works inspired by the tales of pilgrims. Chaucer writes:

> For in their hearts doth Nature stir them so,
> Then people long on pilgrimage go,
> And palmers to be seeking foreign strands,
> To distant shrines renowned in sundry lands.[44]

Goethe (1747–1832) referred to the holy longing as "the desire to be caught up in a deeper quest."[45] Mark Twain (1835–1910) held

---

43. Travel writer and journalist Phil Cousineau compares the longing of the pilgrims' soul to that of the *Pilgrim Astronomer*, a famous sixteenth-century woodcut depicting a man who, "pokes his head through a slit in the dome of the sky so that he might gaze at the machinery behind the sun, stars, and moon and so unveil the mystery of creation (Cousineau, *Art of Pilgrimage*, 50).

44. Chaucer, *Canterbury Tales*, 3.

45. Cited in Cousineau, *Art of Pilgrimage*, 45.

that long journeys provided the possibility of self-improvement;⁴⁶ the twentieth-century poet, T. S. Eliot (1888–1965), described the renewed vision of home as the end of exploration;⁴⁷ and the African American writer, anthropologist, and filmmaker, Zora Neale Hurston (1891–1960), wrote that "travel is the soul of civilization."⁴⁸ These seemingly secular writers helped to bring the spiritual discipline of pilgrimage into the literary realm, illustrating its universal appeal.

This sacralization of travel by secular writers also reiterates the individual's role in determining the meaning of their pilgrimage. Throughout history, pilgrims have defined the significance of their journeys by their personal experiences and in dialogue with the experiences of others.⁴⁹ By sharing these experiences with one another, pilgrims inspire and inform the practices of other pilgrims, embedding a communal element in this otherwise individual act. The universal appeal of pilgrimage, its individualized meaning, and the community created among pilgrims, with its social, political, and ecclesiastical ramifications, brings the practice of the discipline into focus for a conversation of its merits in the twenty-first century and for the postmodern church.

PILGRIMAGE IN THE TWENTY-FIRST CENTURY

The inspiration of former pilgrims has led to the continuation of pilgrimage as a cultural phenomenon into the twenty-first century. Seemingly, Christian travelers continue to recognize God not in a distant heaven but as one that meets them on their journey. However, pilgrimage in the twenty-first century has moved beyond specific sites as the central feature of their journey to an idea of a "third space"—that is any space that transcends societal norms where pilgrims feel a connection to the sacred might become the location

---

46. "[T]ravel is fatal to prejudice, bigotry, and narrow-mindedness" (Twain, *Innocents Abroad*, 407).

47. "We shall not cease from exploration /And the end of all our exploring / Will be to arrive where we started /And know the place for the first time" (Eliot, *Four Quartets*, 49).

48. Cited in Cousineau, *Art of Pilgrimage*, 45.

49. Thomas et al., "To Pray and to Play," 420.

of pilgrimage.[50] While traditional sites such as Rome, Compostela de Santiago, Iona, and Lourdes in France have remained significant sites of Christian pilgrimage, political circumstances have also given rise to new sacred sites.[51] Additional pilgrimage opportunities are connected to no physical site.[52] The experience of the sacred within travel experiences that provide challenge and self-transformation has opened the spiritual discipline to a new world of possibilities.

Pilgrimage has also become linked to, and at times almost indistinguishable from, secular tourism, especially as tourists and pilgrims frequently intersect and interact with one another in their locations of travel.[53] Cousineau attempts to delineate the two, identifying the difference between pilgrim and tourist as "the intention of attention [and] the quality of curiosity."[54] A pilgrim's journey, regardless of location, is toward the center of their universe in search of understanding, spiritual identity, and transformation.

Within this third-space idea, any journey, taken in search of such transformation or understanding, may now, through social construction and sacralization, be considered pilgrimage.[55] As a result, secular sites surrounding famous musical composers and singers, from Beethoven and Wagner to Elvis Presley and Jim Morrison, have become popular destinations of secular pilgrimages.[56] The common feature between these secular sites and the historic understanding of pilgrimage is the use of a destination to commemorate a remembered past and a shared community between

50. Collins-Kreiner, "Researching Pilgrimage," 446.

51. For example, sites in the former USSR attracted pilgrims during a time when pilgrimage was discouraged by the government. In Slovenia, nearly 200 churches are recognized as sites of pilgrimage (Pazos, *Pilgrims and Politics*, 161).

52. Perhaps, similarly, secular pilgrimage can also become about a "thing" rather than a place. Peace Pilgrim, a mystic wanderer in the 1950s and 1960s, wrote: "A pilgrim is a wanderer with a purpose. A pilgrimage can be to a place—that's the best-known kind—but it can also be for a thing. Mine is for peace, and that is why I am Peace Pilgrim" (Pilgrim, *Peace Pilgrim*, 25).

53. Thomas et al., "To Pray and to Play," 413.

54. Cousineau, *Art of Pilgrimage*, 137.

55. Collins-Kreiner, "Researching Pilgrimage," 444.

56. Pazos, *Pilgrims and Politics*, 187.

pilgrims inspired by them. The disconnection of pilgrimage from its spiritual moorings has also opened the discipline to individuals identifying as "spiritual but not religious," which could suggest the benefit of its reclamation by the twenty-first century church.[57] Similarly, secular sites have become the location of sacred pilgrimages. Christian conferences, such as the Passion and Urbana conferences, and the Presbyterian Association of Musicians Worship and Music Conference in Montreat, North Carolina, are examples of Christian pilgrims traveling to sports stadiums and other non-sacred locations for sacred gatherings.[58] Much like pilgrimage in the traditional sense, these events, and the music that accompanies them, have an ability to influence local community practice. The powerful experiences of these conferences in what Monique Ingalls calls, "alternative sacred spaces" enable social experimentation as a result of pilgrimage.[59] Anthropologist Simon Coleman and sociologist Martyn Percy argue that "the 'sacred center' of Protestant pilgrimage comprises not specific places or physical objects, but rather portable practices and discourses intended to be 'transferable' back into more localized ecclesial contexts."[60] These pilgrimages, beyond traditional ecclesial structures and pilgrimage sites, seek a transformational religious experience meant to impact the pilgrim's return to their home community. The common denominator between pilgrims, both sacred and secular, in the twenty-first century is the search for self-transformation, knowledge, and status.[61] Regardless of description, location, or religious connection, they share a common ethos that connects their experiences to those of pilgrims throughout history.

---

57. Lipka and Gecewicz, "More Americans Now Say."
58. Ingalls, "Singing Heaven Down to Earth," 255.
59. Ingalls, "Singing Heaven Down to Earth," 273.
60. Cited in Ingalls, "Singing Heaven Down to Earth," 258.
61. Thomas et al., "To Pray and to Play," 413.

O for a Closer Walk With God

PILGRIMAGE FOR TODAY

As it has increasingly become a "quest without an object," pilgrimage and its impact on individuals and the Christian community are in need of reevaluation.[62] During the period of the late twentieth century and the early decades of the twenty-first century, the discipline has experienced a resurgence, with traditional pilgrimage routes continuing to serve as popular travel destinations and new journeys originating each year. In the mid-1990s, the United Nations released a report suggesting that a rise in pilgrimage practice—the transformative travel to sacred places—would contribute to travel becoming the largest business in the world.[63] Personal transformation, for Christians, as a result of engagement with the material world, suggests that the church may need to look beyond its own walls as it seeks to reach those identifying as "spiritual but not religious" in the twenty-first century.[64] How individuals interact with their surroundings and with others, religious or not, along journeys of self-discovery and transformation, has important consequences for church communities and should shape their connections with their own local communities and the wider world.

Acknowledging this reality, scholars from multiple disciplines have contributed new studies on pilgrimage, seeking to understand the discipline's importance in shaping the narratives of individual pilgrims and faith communities. These studies show that, while connected to a medieval past, pilgrimage is a growing practice for contemporary Christians as they construct meaning *within* their faith tradition. However, it is personal meaning that provides the starting place for understanding postmodern pilgrimage. Richard Niebuhr (1926–2017) said, "Pilgrims are persons in motion—passing through territories not their own—seeking something we might call completion, or perhaps, the word clarity will do as well, a goal to which only the spirit's compass points the way."[65] Pilgrimage, in the twenty-first century, is primarily about self-transformation and

62. Collins-Kreiner, "Researching Pilgrimage," 445.
63. Cousineau, *Art of Pilgrimage*, 13.
64. Frank, "Pilgrimage," 836.
65. Niebuhr, "Pilgrims and Pioneers," 7.

the gaining of knowledge through an experience with the sacred, and it is largely dependent upon the individual's unique and subjective perceptions of what is sacred and their own deeply personal and heterogeneous motivations.[66] The reconciliation of these individual narratives with a church's perception of its own identity may prove to be a challenging venture. Much of the current pilgrimage research indicates that while the church is still a key factor in many pilgrims' construct of meaning it is no longer the defining influencer of most individuals' perceptions. Meaning, then, is subjectively decided by the individual and beyond the church's control on pilgrimage or otherwise.[67] With this in mind, it may be accepted that postmodern pilgrimage is a combination of the individual, with their freedom to construct meaning, with the historical and social practices of pilgrimage, shaped by the church and by previous pilgrims. The historical practices (deep listening, patience, opening of self) and structuring of daily life on pilgrimage continue to be a part of the discipline for postmodern pilgrims.[68] Although historical pilgrimage was focused on penance and healing, these practices are now connected to the liminal moments of personal growth and self-realization for the pilgrim.[69] While initially individualized, these liminal moments do impact the wider culture. As Turner and Turner note, "Liminality provides that generative quality which lends motion to a society by forcing it out of a rigid structure into flowing process."[70] Thus, the personal growth and self-realization of the individual pilgrim has the potential to restructure the society or, in a Christian context, the church. In these moments of liminality, structures and communal values are challenged, suspended, reinterpreted, or replaced. While pilgrimage is largely driven by an individual's motives and construct, its impact in postmodern group contexts has the potential to be far-reaching.

---

66. Thomas et al., "To Pray and to Play," 416.
67. Thomas et al., "To Pray and to Play," 416.
68. Painter, Soul of *a Pilgrim*, 4.
69. Rieger, *Faith on the Road,* 66.
70. Turner and Turner, *Image and Pilgrimage in Christian Culture*, 171.

TOWARD COMMUNITY

In the twenty-first century, there is far greater diversity among pilgrimage participants than at any point in the history of the discipline. Pilgrims now represent those with varying religious affiliations—or none at all. This diversity, along with the rising number of individuals embarking on pilgrimage, has led some scholars to conclude that it is the desire to rediscover the "down-to-earth realities of human beings" that makes pilgrimage a valuable resource in understanding community in the postmodern era.[71] The ease of contemporary travel has made the sites of historical pilgrimage (and perhaps the discipline of pilgrimage) available to a greater diversity of people. As more pilgrims have traveled, more stories, practices, and experiences of their journeys have impacted their home communities. These realities have led to a greater focus on the ways in which pilgrimage might engage entire religious communities, reaching beyond the early focus on pilgrimage sites alone and the later attention to the motivations of individual pilgrims.[72]

The communities of pilgrimage also include the interactions of travelers together.[73] While rituals along the pilgrimage journey might at times mimic or preserve the values of a pilgrim's home community, Turner and Turner's idea that the liminal moments have the ability to reshape the entire society draws attention to the creative and inventive possibilities discovered through the pilgrims' interactions with one another.[74] *Communitas* is realized through the participation of common rituals during the journey. The common rituals have the ability to unite diverse pilgrims when connections of traditional relationships, faith backgrounds, and geographical locations can no longer be assumed.[75] These rituals are well detailed in the writings of pilgrims throughout history and include storytelling and musicmaking.[76] The complex narrative space created at the

---

71. Pazos, *Pilgrims and Politics*, 2.
72. Frank, "Pilgrimage," 835.
73. Ingalls, "Singing Heaven Down to Earth," 255.
74. Kubicki, *Liturgical Music as Ritual Symbol*, 132.
75. Rieger, *Faith on the Road*, 70.
76. Bohlman, "Pilgrimage."

intersection of the individual pilgrim's motivation and construct, the common rituals, and the community formed through music is the essence of what the discipline might contribute to the postmodern church.[77] In this postmodern understanding, the pilgrim does not lose their individuality in the formation of community on the journey but rather contributes to the unique dynamics of shared experience, with music serving as one catalyst for the formation of that relationship.

Musicmaking provides one significant way that pilgrims form community, respond to the journey, and work for the transformation that motivated their journey. The songs of their journey become an expansion of their individual pilgrimage stories that impact both the temporary community of their pilgrimage and their communities back home. While ethnomusicologists have focused on the role of music as mediator between sacred space and physical space[78] this limited focus fails to recognize the role of music and ritual in the overall pilgrimage experience.[79] Pilgrimage song reflects an important ritual and storytelling component that deserves further consideration as the benefits of pilgrimage in the postmodern era are considered.

Chapter 3 will explore the role of music in pilgrimage throughout history and for the postmodern era.

---

77. Bohlman, "Final Borderpost," 447.
78. Ingalls, "Singing Heaven Down to Earth," 257–58.
79. Bohlman, "Final Borderpost," 430.

3

Be My Song as I Journey
The Role of Music on Pilgrimage

Lord Jesus, you shall be my song as I journey;
I'll tell everybody about you wherever I go:
you alone are our life and our peace and our love.
Lord Jesus, you shall be my song as I journey.[1]

THE ROLE OF MUSIC ON PILGRIMAGE

Music has a multifaceted role along the pilgrimage journey, serving as inspiration and a transformational mediator, storyteller, and community-builder. The songs of pilgrims have also played an important part in the dissemination of the pilgrimage discipline throughout history and continue to shape the pilgrimage experience of the postmodern context. Richard R. Niebuhr said, "Pilgrims are poets who create by taking journeys."[2] While music may be a pilgrim's creative output following pilgrimage, it also serves an important function during the journey as it helps to create meaning

---

1. Text © Les Petites Soeurs de Jésus/English translation ©1970 Stephen Somerville (admin. Augsburg Fortress). Used by Permission.

2. Niebuhr, "Pilgrims and Pioneers," 7.

for the pilgrim, connects to the past, narrates the journey, and helps to fashion a new story and reality for the individual and the wider pilgrimage group.

Music on pilgrimage is both an individual and communal experience. Studying the musicmaking of pilgrimage offers the opportunity to examine the relationship between pilgrims as they negotiate their individual quests for self-transformation and their relationship to and with one another.[3] Pilgrimage, like art and poetry, is concerned with meaning at each stage of the journey.[4] The music of the pilgrimage is one medium through which this meaning is created or transformed. Pilgrimage accounts demonstrate that music may be created at any stage of the journey—either through the process of composition or through the sharing of songs among travelers. This music defines the experience for the individual, is embedded in the practice of the community, and will help to retell the story upon the pilgrim's return.[5] The meaning of the music, indeed even the songs themselves, is not static but rather constantly changing as it is performed by different individuals, used along the journey, and recreated by others.[6] The song of pilgrimage is an embodied act of faith. Thus, it is only in the performance of the songs that they have meaning.

Because the music of pilgrimage requires performance by the pilgrims, the songs of the journey must enable the active participation of the group traveling together. This is not only a pragmatic concern but also an act of hospitality as pilgrims come into community with one another. The inclusive nature of pilgrimage music requires structures and forms that are conducive to a wide diversity of performers. The repertoires are frequently multilingual and adaptable to the specific contexts and traditions of the pilgrimage group.[7] An example of this practice is the specific form of music used by the ecumenical community at Taizé to foster community

---

3. Wood, "Soundscapes of Pilgrimage," 285.
4. Cousineau, *Art of Pilgrimage*, 160.
5. Bohlman, "Final Borderpost," 436.
6. Bohlman, "Final Borderpost," 442.
7. Bohlman, "Final Borderpost," 441–42.

among pilgrims from all over the world.[8] Often short, cyclical songs available in multiple languages make the music of pilgrimage immediately accessible to a diverse group of people gathering for the first time.

Again, the Psalms of Ascent provide an important biblical and historical reference for how music on pilgrimage bridges the gap between the individual and the group. Psalms were frequently used by pilgrims to "infuse courage into the hearts" of the individuals and link them together upon their departure.[9] The Psalms of Ascent (120–134) contain texts written in the first person singular (120–23, 130, 131), second person (127, 128), and first person plural (125, 126, 132–34), illustrating the nature of pilgrimage as both individual act and communal experience. The recitation of these psalms, either by singing or speaking, becomes a corporate act of prayer, unifying the pilgrims into a cohesive unit.[10]

The unification of pilgrims by and through musicmaking is a characteristic of pilgrimage across religious and geographical bounds. M. J. Sallnow notes in his studies of pilgrims in the Andes Mountains that, "without ritual dancers [and music], the purpose of a pilgrimage could not be fulfilled."[11] For diasporic Tamil Hindus, musicmaking is the singular action that allows the group to become one again when they gather from the many places of their forced migration around the world.[12] The music of pilgrimage serves as a catalyst for the construction of meaning by pilgrims and for the development of community among them.

Because of this need to connect a diverse group of people, pilgrimage collections have historically relied on familiar forms such as strophic hymns or cyclical songs with repetitive patterns.[13] For many pilgrims, the music of their journey consists of a common

---

8. Kubicki, "Taizé (USA)."
9. Cousineau, *Art of Pilgrimage,* 100.
10. Cousins, "Conversing," 41.
11. Sallnow, "Communitas Reconsidered," 171.
12. Hornabrook, "Songs of the Saints," 117.
13. Bohlman, "Pilgrimage."

core of songs supplemented by pilgrimage-specific collections.[14] These collections, like the Psalms of Ascent, demonstrate how familiar structures, texts, and melodies may be used to link individuals together into a common community even within the new context of their journeying. Like the pilgrimage discipline itself, this music and the musicmaking of the pilgrims often falls outside the bounds of traditional religious repertoires and canonical practices.[15] The musical genres and sources of pilgrims are diverse and consist of devotional music brought from home, the music of others, and the experience of a wider soundscape in the destination of their journey.[16] The music of their experience is not overly concerned with the musical orthodoxy of the church but rather with the connection it creates between the diverse pilgrims. Music becomes the vehicle by which the diverse cultural backgrounds and contexts of individual pilgrims meld into a shared experience. Philip Bohlman notes: "Music enables the crossing of political and linguistic borders often required in sacred journeys, further inculcating pilgrimage repertoires with political significance."[17] In this process, music helps to create a new sociopolitical reality for pilgrims.

While it may not be music alone that creates this new political reality, music is capable of transmitting meaning and understanding if approached from a new hermeneutical paradigm.[18] This is essential to considering the ways in which the pilgrimage discipline and its music might be used in the reformation of political and ecclesiastical structures in the postmodern era. The ideas and music of pilgrimage have the ability to influence and shape practices and beliefs at the local level.[19] The new community formed as a result of the music of pilgrimage is one that combines elements of what has come before, the story of the journey itself, and the new song that is produced through the interactions of diverse pilgrims along the way.

14. In Europe, the *Marienlob* is one such collection (Bohlman, "Final Borderpost," 433).

15. Bohlman, "Final Borderpost," 435.

16. Wood, "Soundscapes of Pilgrimage," 287.

17. Bohlman, "Pilgrimage," para. 4.

18. Kubicki, *Liturgical Music as Ritual Symbol*, 41–42.

19. Ingalls, "Singing Heaven Down to Earth," 273.

Be My Song as I Journey

PILGRIMAGE MUSIC AS CONNECTION TO THE PAST

The music of pilgrimage has provided one of the best records of sacred journeying and, by extension, has become a means for recording history.[20] The embodied songs of pilgrims connect their current experience to the stories of those gone before and open the possibility for future pilgrims to share in this common history. In Judeo-Christian contexts, this is again highlighted by the Psalms of Ascent. These psalms are simultaneously a three-way conversation between God, the pilgrim, and the rest of the pilgrimage group. The texts, from God in the past, invite conversation with God and with one another about God in the present experience, hopefully informing and shaping a new reality.[21] The music of pilgrimage provides for the historical, spatial, transnational, spiritual, communal, and individual experience of the pilgrim.[22] These songs bring an element of home into the journey toward the sacred and hoped-for transformation. However, on the journey these practices cross paths with songs of other pilgrims and the communities through which pilgrims travel, producing a new song that is some hybrid of these different worlds.[23]

Historically, the individual songs of pilgrimage focused on themes related to the location of the pilgrimage and/or the saint/miracle associated with that site as well as a shared history with previous pilgrims. As pilgrims brought elements of home into their musical repertoire, common Western European ideas of harmony, silence, and beauty became a part of these historical collections.[24] However, the convergence of these ideas with other songs and musical ideas produced a new modified folksong. Using the term "folk music" to describe the music of pilgrimage implies that the community is actively engaged with the music.[25] This engagement

20. Bohlman, "Pilgrimage, Politics," 376.
21. Cousins, "Conversing," 41.
22. Hornabrook, "Songs of the Saints," 108.
23. Wood, "Soundscapes of Pilgrimage," 287.
24. Wood, "Soundscapes of Pilgrimage," 288.
25. Kubicki, *Liturgical Music as Ritual Symbol,* 54.

with the song, along with the intersection of different individuals and communities, produces a new product rooted in the past but uniquely different. With the ease of travel in the twenty-first century and the growing racial, ethnic, geographical, and religious backgrounds of individuals undertaking pilgrimage, the folk music of pilgrimage will assume a similar diversity.

The characteristics of any individual pilgrim song may no longer be of primary importance when considering music as the connection to the past. While these learned songs connect to that past, it is the performative nature of these pieces and their connection to the social and political contexts of the present pilgrimage group that make them relevant for postmodern discussion. This broader understanding suggests that any song might function as a song of pilgrimage if it narrates a shared history with previous pilgrims, is relevant to the current group, and allows for the experience of pilgrimage to be shared at its conclusion with others through its subsequent performance.[26] Like their reasons for departing on pilgrimage, individuals bring their own musical identities to the pilgrimage experience but continue to be anchored by a common historical and spiritual past that shapes the retelling of their own pilgrimage experiences.[27] The music of pilgrimage becomes, then, an important narrator for the journey, connecting the history of home and the experiences of past pilgrims with the current pilgrimage and, hopefully, to a new, transformed future.

PILGRIMAGE MUSIC AS NARRATOR ON THE JOURNEY

The music of pilgrimage serves an important role in narrating the steps of the journey for the individual pilgrim and the collective group. Music's narrativity charts the way and shapes the worldview of the pilgrim and provides a ritual practice to accompany important moments of the experience. The pilgrim's attention to intention makes the creation of music along the way akin to an act of

26. Bohlman, "Pilgrimage."
27. Thomas et al., "To Pray and to Play," 420.

prayer and joins other practices or rituals as an essential part of the pilgrim's journey.[28] Music becomes a narrative space that leads the pilgrim from the point of departure to the sacred destination and mediates the encounter with the divine. This important function of pilgrimage music requires that some music/rituals be learned prior to the journey.[29] The prior knowledge and practice of the ritual allows the pilgrim to be fully present in the liminal space of the journey.[30] However, as pilgrims move, group dynamics change, and music encounters the different communities of pilgrimage, the ritual of music will adapt to the specific context of any given journey.

While the music of pilgrimage plays a functional role in narrating the journey, it also becomes a significant aspect of the pilgrimage in and of itself. Song gives the pilgrim the ritual necessary for mediating a sacred moment but also has the power to become *the* central moment of pilgrimage. The performance of music may become a form of sung pilgrimage, connecting the singer to a network of sacred and secular experiences.[31] While not a literal journey, music has the ability to become a metaphorical pilgrimage, connected to home through songs previously learned but experienced in a sacred moment available only through and mediated by the music. This phenomenon allows music to become an almost mystical speech for former pilgrims to use in remembering their experience when sharing it with those who have not had the same experience. This mystical speech, required if a pilgrimage moment is to achieve its desired goal, sacralizes music for the individual pilgrim, uniting their experience with the divine.[32] It is the combination of the learned music brought by the pilgrim with the experience of the journey that gives way to a unique, sacred phenomenon found only through their song.

Not surprisingly, however, the group shares some role and responsibility in this sacred moment. Since the music must be

---

28. Painter, *Soul of a Pilgrim*, 15–17.
29. Cited in Cousineau, *Art of Pilgrimage*, 155.
30. Turner and Turner, *Image and Pilgrimage in Christian Culture*, 171.
31. Hornabrook, "Songs of the Saints," 108.
32. Bohlman, "Final Borderpost," 440.

performed to have meaning, pilgrimage music is dependent upon the shared performance of the pilgrimage community. Pilgrims, most having met each other for the first time along their journey, often use music as a way to find commonality with one another and to define their common goals.[33] The intersections and compromising between individual pilgrims yields important insights. The sharing of contexts, meanings, and goals links the individuals, while also giving a glimpse into what communal values are shared, indexed, and encouraged within the group. These values will also be used to transmit the meaning of the journey upon the pilgrims' return to their respective homes.[34] Music becomes the tool by which pilgrim communities define themselves and, because of the inclusive structures of the music, all members of the group share in crafting that definition. Relationships *and* meaning are defined through the performance of the songs on the journey.[35]

The music of pilgrimage may take place at any point along the journey. Thus, any moment along the way has the potential of becoming sacred.[36] This reality imbues the entirety of the pilgrimage experience—the individual contexts and reasons for embarkment, the relationships shared, the moment of departure, the journey itself, as well as the arrival and return—with sacredness. It is these encounters, experienced through the modified music of pilgrimage, that craft the new, transformed story of the pilgrim. The discipline of pilgrimage then becomes cyclical as these stories are shared, upon return, with future pilgrims.

PILGRIMAGE MUSIC AS THE NEW STORY

While pilgrimage song is the narration of the journey connected to a shared history, it also becomes a communicator of the new story and reality of the transformed pilgrim. As the individual members of the pilgrimage community interact, define their values, and sing

33. Bohlman, "Final Borderpost," 435.
34. Ingalls, "Singing Heaven Down to Earth," 259–60.
35. Stokes, "Travel and Tourism," 149.
36. Thomas et al., "To Pray and to Play," 419.

together, the hoped-for transformation of their journey becomes a communal event where their shared music is a corporate expression of that transformation.[37] The implication of the shared musical expression by the pilgrimage community is that the pilgrim needs connection with God *and* the community to experience the benefits of their own transformation.

The music of these interactions is as diverse as the pilgrims themselves—what might be compared to a modern-day Pentecost—an amalgamation of the different languages, liturgies, and contexts of the individuals that engage in this discipline. This reality is not without challenge as individuals encounter "the other," juxtaposing their own preconceptions, practices, and music with those of the wider community.[38] An eschatological awareness seems to pervade pilgrims' impressions of this experience as Monique Ingalls notes about evangelical Christians: "The experience of being part of a vast gathering of Christians singing together . . . is used to interpret biblical accounts of the ideal community at the end of time."[39] This diversity of input, experience, and connection to the "ideal community" shapes the individual pilgrim's viewpoint and hope for the future as they return from their journey.[40]

As has been discussed earlier, pilgrimage has an immediate impact on the communities of the traveler. The desired outcome of pilgrimage is that the image of the ideal community becomes a guidepost by which the pilgrims approach all future encounters. Music provides one means by which the spiritual ideas of the pilgrimage journey might intersect with daily life upon return.[41] The music of pilgrimage may allow the pilgrim to experience a feeling of transcendence—a crossing of the material world with the spiritual world—that results in a deeper understanding and experience of the present life.[42] These transcendent experiences enable participants to

---

37. Cousins, "Conversing," 46.
38. Wood, "Soundscapes of Pilgrimage," 289.
39. Ingalls, "Singing Heaven Down to Earth," 263.
40. Wood, "Soundscapes of Pilgrimage," 295.
41. Bohlman, "Final Borderpost," 427.
42. Hornabrook, "Songs of the Saints," 138.

realize the imagined community, with its expressions, actions, and music, thus making heaven accessible in the here and now.[43] The diversity of these songs also allows pilgrims to move beyond the confines of their pre-rehearsed roles and texts and the orthodoxy of their individual contexts. As the song is transformed through the encounters of pilgrimage, the pilgrims' image of the transcendent is broadened with cultural barriers broken through the performance of their shared song.[44] These experiences create a new world and reality for the pilgrim that moves from what is to what could be.

The initial reasons for undertaking pilgrimage often illustrate the ways in which a pilgrim is seeking something beyond the comfortable realities of their current world. The music of pilgrimage breaks down these preconceived ideas and demonstrates how the pilgrim's transformation may be dependent upon the broadening of their worldview or possibly the obfuscation of their current ideas.[45] The eclectic encounters with the other and the formation of a new song through their shared experiences contributes to the broadening of view for the individual pilgrim which may raise awareness of systemic issues and concerns for justice and reconciliation in their home communities.[46] The pilgrims' songs have the potential to become a political act, standing in the face of the status quo. Their wider repertoire, employed to include the songs of everyone, including the poor and oppressed, offers a glimpse of heaven on earth that changes the pilgrims' outlook for society.[47] Brazilian scholar Suzel Ana Reily characterizes this shift in perspective:

> Through musical performance, religious discourse and aesthetic experience become inextricably intertwined, inclining participants to experience the ritual space as an encounter with the moral order of the sacred. In such an enchanted world, participants construct and

---

43. Ingalls, "Singing Heaven Down to Earth," 263.
44. Bohlman, "Final Borderpost," 450.
45. Bohlman, "Final Borderpost," 441.
46. Ingalls, "Singing Heaven Down to Earth," 275.
47. Hawn, *New Songs of Celebration Render*, 314.

simultaneously experience the harmonious order that could reign in their society.[48]

The embodied performance of pilgrimage music then inscribes new possibilities for the pilgrim's future home.

In the twentieth century, several ecumenical communities have looked to the music of the pilgrims that gather in their midst as foundational, at least partially, to their identities.[49] The influence of the Taizé and Iona communities are of particular importance as their music and liturgical resources have been published and made accessible for pilgrims and other communities around the world. These communities, drawing tens of thousands of sacred travelers to their locations each year, provide important case studies for considering the ways in which music builds communities, changes social constructs, and transforms pilgrims within their communities. Chapter 4 will explore the history, dynamics, and role of music for these pilgrimage communities and how their influence on the wider church could shape a new reality in the postmodern world.

---

48. Reily, *Voices of the Magi*, 17.
49. Hawn, *New Songs of Celebration Render*, 302.

4

Will You Come and Follow Me?

The Ecumenical Communities of Iona and Taizé—Case Studies of the Modern Pilgrimage

Lord, your summons echoes true when you but call my name.
Let me turn and follow you and never be the same.
In your company I'll go where you love and footsteps show.
Thus I'll move and live and grow in you and you in me.[1]

THE HISTORY AND IMPACT OF THE ECUMENICAL COMMUNITY AT TAIZÉ

Founded in 1949 by Brother Roger Louis Schutz-Marsauche (1915–2005), the ecumenical community located in Taizé, France (hereafter referred to as the Taizé Community) has a long history of welcoming pilgrims from around the world and employing music as a means for extending hospitality, building community, and shaping transformative moments for their visitors. While not originally established to be a site of pilgrimage, the thousands of

---

1. Bell & Maule, "The Summons," Stanza 5. © 1987 Wild Goose Resource Group, Iona Community (admin. GIA Publications, Inc.).

individuals from four continents who travel to Taizé each year connect the community to the pilgrimage discipline.[2]

One of the first Protestant monastic orders in history, the Taizé brothers are committed to "reconciliation through prayer" in their life together, which is guided by a common rule and a commitment to daily worship.[3] From their earliest beginnings, the community became a place of hospitality for spiritual seekers, including Jewish refugees during World War II. In his authoritative work on the early history of Taizé, José Luis González Balado describes Brother Roger's twofold vision to be "a community that prays, rooting all its life in contemplation, and a place where the generations meet, where the young are made welcome."[4] Through their commitment to providing hospitality, the Taizé Community opened monastic practices to a wider, more ecumenical church.[5] By the early 1970s, nearly 60,000 young pilgrims were traveling to Taizé on an annual basis challenging the original ideas and structures Brother Roger had created for the burgeoning organization.[6]

The brothers of the community came to understand that their forms of prayer, music, living, and worship space would need to adapt in order to accommodate the large number of pilgrims.[7] This adaptability would become a defining characteristic of the group. Changes to the worship order presented a deeply personal issue for the brothers—would they continue employing the daily prayer services they had used since their inception, or would they change the prayers to better integrate the visitors into the worship experience?[8] The modern structure of the Taizé prayers (and the musical form

---

2. Kubicki, *Liturgical Music as Ritual Symbol*, 130.

3. Hawn, *New Songs of Celebration Render*, 303.

4. Balado, Story of *Taizé*, 7–8. Readers interested in a longer history than this book will allow should seek out this book for a more comprehensive background of Brother Roger and the early years of the Taizé Community.

5. Santos, *Community Called Taizé*, 63.

6. Santos, *Community Called Taizé*, 71.

7. One example of this was the use of a large circus tent to accommodate additional people when the Church of Reconciliation, the community's primary gathering space, became too small for the growing crowds.

8. Santos, *Community Called Taizé*, 106.

closely associated with them) developed gradually over time. An early prayer book, consisting mostly of edited daily worship orders from the Lutheran and Reformed traditions, had been developed by Brother Roger in 1977 and laid out the basic foundations for the community's worshiping life: "to worship God and to express the fact that our communion with Him is social as our humanity itself is social."[9] For Roger, it was this social element that made adapting the liturgy and music to welcome pilgrims essential.

The brothers gradually substituted what had been sacred and traditional for them for that which was accessible to the wider group. The Bible readings used in worship were shortened, different languages were used, and the songs of worship simplified—eventually leading to the Taizé chants discussed later in this chapter.[10] Brother Roger also developed a new lectionary, believing that the pilgrims, often young or new Christians, needed readings that introduced the most fundamental aspects of the faith.[11] Still in use today, these pericopes are also used in the Bible introductions and sharing group sessions that are substantial components of the pilgrims' daily life at Taizé. All of these modifications demonstrate the ways in which the Taizé Community continually negotiates the differences between their own identity and the identities of the pilgrims they welcome. Even today, the brothers seek to find common elements that link everyone together during the prayers, with music playing a significant role in that task.[12] The shared experiences of pilgrims and the brothers continue to make Taizé a significant place of pilgrimage and holy encounter in the twenty-first century.

---

9. Cited in Kubicki, *Liturgical Music as Ritual Symbol*, 137.
10. Hawn, *New Songs of Celebration Render*, 305.
11. Santos, *Community Called Taizé*, 112.
12. Kubicki, *Liturgical Music as Ritual Symbol*, 138.

Figure 2: Taizé block altar and sails, Image © 2008 by the Taizé Community. Used with permission.

The work of the community continues today with approximately 100 brothers carrying on the ideas of Brother Roger and the original group.[13] While the membership of the brothers does include some ordained Catholic priests and Protestant pastors, it is mostly comprised of nonordained men. Since its beginning, the group has existed outside of the structure of any organized church, allowing for a distinctly different experience than home for most pilgrims.[14] The active participation of those pilgrims in worship remains a high priority for the brothers.[15]

The disconnection from their ordinary lives and church structures and the active participation encouraged by the brothers at Taizé affords pilgrims a liminal space where unity and an experience of *communitas* may happen.[16] The collective prayers of the different groups gathered together provide the location and performative action required to give meaning to the pilgrimage experience as

13. Hawn, *New Songs of Celebration Render*, 303.
14. Santos, *Community Called Taizé*, 81.
15. Kubicki, *Liturgical Music as Ritual Symbol*, 46.
16. Kubicki, *Liturgical Music as Ritual Symbol*, 145.

outlined in chapter 3. For many, it is the music of Taizé that plays the pivotal role in allowing this diverse group to pray together.

THE MUSIC OF THE TAIZÉ COMMUNITY

The common prayers of the Taizé Community are centered in singing and silence. The singing portion of the services, held three times per day, has evolved throughout the group's history. Initially, the community drew music from the traditions of the brothers—primarily from Reformed and Lutheran sources.[17] However, the goal of enabling all who gathered to participate in the prayers quickly necessitated the creation of new music. Brother Robert, who joined the order in 1946, is credited with the idea for what would become known as the Taizé chants.[18] As early as the 1960s, the brothers expressed a desire to utilize music in the prayers that would facilitate the inclusion of the diverse pilgrims in their worship.[19] The chants that developed were primarily focused on enabling the active participation of all in worship, not on creating a new musical or liturgical form, but on bringing young people from different backgrounds into a common form of prayer.

Although the brothers were most interested in creating music that enabled the active participation of all in worship, they were also concerned about the quality of the music offered. For the community, liturgical music needed to consist of both quality texts and quality music.[20] The composition of the chants began in 1974, when Brother Robert, preparing for Taizé's first Council of Youth, realized he needed music that would encourage the participation of a large, diverse group of people from across the world. After the successful use of Michael Praetorius's canon, *Jubilate Deo*, Robert believed that other similar music might be used in the prayers. He held that this music must consist of "original compositions of solid quality that can be used by the people of God . . . and in this sense be

17. Hawn, *New Songs of Celebration Render*, 304.
18. Hawn, *New Songs of Celebration Render*, 305.
19. Santos, *Community Called Taizé*, 104.
20. Kubicki, *Liturgical Music as Ritual Symbol*, 49.

called *popular.*"[21] Robert employed well-known French composer and church musician Jacques Berthier to assist in this endeavor. Robert would compile texts for Berthier and often guided the composer's process, offering comments and revisions along the way.[22] Robert was also charged with teaching this form of sung prayer to the gathered worshippers. These compositions were often written in Latin because of its history as the language of the church and the common link it provided for the diverse worshippers.[23] As this musical form developed and the large groups of pilgrims diversified, the songs were provided in multiple languages in the Church of Reconciliation, with individuals encouraged to sing in their own native tongue.

The singing of the Taizé chants in multiple languages allows each individual to encounter the other in the prayers. The multiple languages employed, or the use of the unspoken Latin by the entire assembly, allows the music to serve as community-builder in the experience, creating a liminal space shared by the diverse assembly. Jason Brian Santos notes about this shared liminal space, "[this encounter with] our neighbor forces us to put aside our own pride and ideologies and focus on what is central to all Christians."[24] In setting aside their own ideologies, the pilgrims are opened to a new worldview as a result of the Taizé music. These songs, encountered on their individual pilgrimage journeys, invite the pilgrims into a shared community through their active participation in the simple forms of the Taizé chants. Like the pilgrimage music discussed in chapter 3, these songs transform and take on different meanings for each new group of pilgrims, performing them both at Taizé and around the world. These meanings shape the new story of the pilgrims who sing them, hopefully impacting their own communities.

---

21. Cited in Kubicki, *Liturgical Music as Ritual Symbol,* 52 (emphasis original).

22. Kubicki, *Liturgical Music as Ritual Symbol,* 48.

23. Hawn, *New Songs of Celebration Render,* 306.

24. Santos, *Community Called Taizé,* 129.

From *Plague* to *Purpose*

THE GLOBAL IMPACT OF THE TAIZÉ COMMUNITY

As the Taizé Community continues to grow and change in the twenty-first century, so have their efforts to reach the diverse pilgrim population that finds meaning through their form of music and prayer. This outreach has extended to include international events, which the brothers call "pilgrimages of trust," in locations around the world. The Community continues to understand itself as "a starting point for young pilgrims" and seeks to provide inspiration and resources for young seekers exploring their faith.[25] The Taizé chants provide a freedom of worship expression that is known for its ability to create relationship among a diverse group of people while also allowing individuals to move toward God and transformation at their own pace.[26] The community's form of worship and song has impacted not only the lives of pilgrims who have visited Taizé but also the worship lives of Christian communities around the world.

Through their pilgrimages of trust and their publication efforts, the Taizé chants have now been disseminated throughout the Christian church. Their impact in the United States has been particularly profound due to their highly successful agreement with GIA Music Publications to market and sell their worship materials. As Michael Hawn notes about the impact of Taizé, "to many worshipers in the United States, prayer in the Taizé Community with fewer words and extended periods of silence may be at once disorienting and refreshing."[27] With the music of Taizé now included in many mainline, Protestant denominational hymnals, the re-created story of pilgrims has had an impact on the practice of local communities. Regardless of its success, the experience of Taizé worship has caused pilgrims' home congregations to consider how their worship offers space for individuals to pursue God through silence and simplified musical forms, embedding aspects of the pilgrimage discipline into their local liturgical practices.

25. Santos, *Community Called Taizé*, 21.
26. Santos, *Community Called Taizé*, 139.
27. Hawn, *New Songs of Celebration Render*, 304.

In considering the continued influence of pilgrimage and the Taizé Community's ability to shape their own identity based on the needs and experiences of the pilgrims, the Taizé chants stand as a strong example of how the discipline might reshape the postmodern church. As Jason Brian Santos notes:

> Through [the brothers'] quest for reconciliation we are privileged to witness one of their most inspiring and admirable qualities in action: adaptability. In their development as a community they have consistently listened and adapted to the call of God upon their collective life.[28]

This adaptability, especially as seen in their preferred musical form, suggests the innate ability of pilgrimage to reshape the story of both the individual pilgrim's life and that of an entire community.

THE HISTORY AND IMPACT OF THE IONA COMMUNITY

For centuries the island of Iona, off the western coast of Scotland, has been a beacon of pilgrimage and religious activity, attracting tens of thousands of travelers—including church leaders, unemployed teenagers, theologians, workers, tourists, and pilgrims—each year.[29]

The history and impact of the modern Iona Community is unquestionably linked to that of this remote island. George MacLeod's (1895–1991) social experiment, begun in 1938 and later known as the Iona Community, stands as the latest chapter in the long history of this place.

In the Christian tradition, the arrival of the Irish monk Colum Cille, later known as St. Columba, in 563 CE provided the impetus for Iona's monastic heritage and its importance as a site of pilgrimage and inspiration for contemporary movements.[30] However, the

---

28. Santos, *Community Called Taizé*, 54.
29. Ferguson, *Chasing the Wild Goose*, 15.
30. Bentley, "Community, Authenticity, Growth," 72.

island's name, which means the "island of yew,"[31] suggests that Iona may have been a significant sacred place for non-Christian traditions prior to Columba's arrival.[32] The popular legend holds that Columba, a well-educated Irish monk, made an illegal copy of the Latin Vulgate with plans to keep it for himself. Facing legal charges, he fled Ireland, landing on Iona on the eve of Pentecost. While it is likely that Columba returned to Ireland several times after landing on Iona, his travel to the island, where he built the first abbey and established a Christian monastic community, was considered a form of exile—keeping with the Irish tradition of a making a sacrificial journey for Christ's sake and connected to the interior journey of the soul.[33] His journey mimics the traditional pattern of medieval pilgrims who left the safety of their own economic and social contexts in search of divine inspiration.

Columba's exile was one of the essential features of the Irish ascetic life and of Celtic spirituality. The discipline of peregrination (wandering or pilgrimage) was a significant practice in Ireland, and Columba and his monks became collectively known as the Peregrini—the wanderers.[34] Within this Celtic tradition, pilgrims, who often went to islands or to live in caves, led monastic lives which held freedom and discipline in tension with one another. As Ian Bradley notes in his biography of Columba: "he was part pilgrim, part penitent, and part politician."[35] These characteristics defined the monk's life and work on the island and provide the connection between Columba's Iona and the work of the contemporary Iona Community.[36] Columba's example, the life and work of his monks, and the island itself have fascinated Christian seekers, musicians, and artists into the twenty-first century and provided inspiration for the Iona Community and, through their work, pilgrims around the world.

31. According to the *Oxford Dictionary*, a yew is a type of evergreen tree often linked with folklore and superstition.
32. Power, "Place of Community," 37.
33. Ferguson, *Chasing the Wild Goose*, 23.
34. Ferguson, *Chasing the Wild Goose*, 25, 31.
35. Bradley, *Columba*, 23.
36. Hawn, *New Songs of Celebration Render*, 308.

From its earliest days, Iona was a location of religious diversity and a mixture of cultures. Due to this, it has always been a place where people of different backgrounds and lifestyles lived together—negotiating their individual sense of freedom with the need to belong to the island community.[37] This history, the hope of rediscovering the ideas that informed Columba's monastic life, and the desire for a rhythm of life different from societal norms and the common orthodoxy of the church inspired George MacLeod, a Church of Scotland pastor, to found the modern-day Iona Community. MacLeod, frustrated by what he perceived as the Scottish seminaries' inability to prepare ministerial candidates for service in the poor neighborhoods of Glasgow, had an ambitious idea to rebuild the medieval abbey on the island which had been in ruins for many years. Pairing young ministers and candidates for ministry with out-of-work craftsmen, MacLeod's idea was an experiment in community. The men employed, a mixture of clergy and laity, lived together, worshipped together, and worked together for three to four months each summer.[38] This experiment was rooted in the idea that Christianity was a community-based faith and that the church was failing to provide such a community. MacLeod believed that the individual was called to discipleship within the context of a supporting and demanding community and the current state of the church required a new approach.[39] The Iona Community, from the beginning, has been rooted in community-building and accountability to one another.

While the modern community is not ascetic in the manner of Columba, its members still adhere to a rule of life with financial, communal, and daily worship commitments that distinguish it from society.[40] This common rule is inspired by the monastic life at the heart of the abbey's history. As MacLeod remarked, "as we looked at the abbey, we were reminded that the whole purpose of

---

37. Power, "Place of Community," 35.
38. Hawn, *New Songs of Celebration Render*, 311.
39. Ferguson, *Chasing the Wild Goose*, 125.
40. Hawn, *New Songs of Celebration Render*, 308.

the experiment was to prove that what it stood for still worked."[41] The rule continues to inform the lives of the members of the Iona Community, scattered throughout Europe, as well as the daily pattern of life at the Iona Island Centre. For the workers, the daily routine included morning worship, work, hymn practice, and evening worship.[42] This pattern continues with resident staff, members, and guests participating in twice-daily worship (which the community refers to as services), "big sings," and common work to this day.

As the Iona Community grew and the reconstruction of the abbey concluded, the community's purpose became increasingly about providing a place of study, group learning, and training in discipleship for the wider church. Committed to diversity and radical hospitality, the community adopted an ethos that favored questions rather than answers—a position that dramatically shaped the abbey's music and worship life.[43] The group continues to be influenced by MacLeod's vision for a shared common life and his desire that Iona be a place for questioning and challenging faith that shapes the future lives of pilgrims once they return home.[44] The sculpture of "The Descent of the Spirit" located in the cloisters of the abbey, visually captures this focus on a different future. The sculpture, a controversial addition when MacLeod received it from a Texas donor, depicts the Virgin Mary being birthed from a heart made up of three parts held together by the beak of a descending dove. As Ronald Ferguson, a former leader of the group, notes, "this modern sign gathers up the ancient, still scandalous, theme of incarnation and throws the imagination forward into the future."[45] With an eye toward a radical future, the Iona Community continues to welcome guests and seeks to build community among the many diverse pilgrims who find their way to the rocky shore of the island each year. This pilgrimage community is formed with the hope of influencing and shaping practices within the wider church.

---

41. Ferguson, *Chasing the Wild Goose*, 392.
42. Power, "Place of Community," 39.
43. Ferguson, *Chasing the Wild Goose*, 110.
44. Ferguson, *Chasing the Wild Goose*, 103.
45. Ferguson, *Chasing the Wild Goose*, 152.

Figure 3: "Descent of the Holy Spirit" by Jacques Lipchitz

In welcoming these individuals, the Iona Community stresses the fact that the abbey is not a retreat center. Rather, it is a place for encounter and personal and social transformation through the rediscovery of a common life. It is the aim of the community that this rediscovery might subsequently result in the renewal of church in pilgrims' own communities.[46] Again, the history of the island influences this work. From the islanders who have always been dependent on one another for survival, the Benedictines, and the current-day Iona Community, the experience of the holy on the island has been found in togetherness and hospitality, a sacred

46. Bentley, "Community, Authenticity, Growth," 72.

monastic obligation. Ferguson notes, "hospitality was sacred, because Christ was in the stranger."[47] The Gaelic Rune of Hospitality remains a hallmark text for the community:

> I saw a stranger yestreen:
> I put food in the eating place,
> Drink in the drinking place,
> Music in the listening place:
> And in the sacred name of the Triune
> He blessed myself and my house,
> My cattle and my dear ones.
> And the lark said in her son
> Often, often, often
> Goes the Christ in the stranger's guise.[48]

MacLeod places this objective in much simpler terms: "we do not seek Christ in the ruins, we find him in the fellowship."[49] For the Iona Community, hospitality and the common life are essential elements of a faithful Christian life which is personal but also needs communal support. For MacLeod and the future iterations of the community, this was (and continues to be) the problem facing the church—how to live corporately while also understanding, supporting, and respecting the individual. They believe the church, and more specifically the worship of the church, must find a way to bridge the gap between Sunday mornings and the everyday lives of the individuals. This is reflected in the radical approach the community takes in their understandings of daily worship, the liturgy, music, and its role in forming community among pilgrims and sustaining individuals when they return to their own homes.

The intersection of worship, work, and learning have been at the heart of the community's understanding of themselves since the beginning. The music and liturgy of the organization, different in structure from the strident order of the Church of Scotland, have long attracted pilgrims to their work.[50] For MacLeod and his abbey

---

47. Ferguson, *Chasing the Wild Goose*, 25.
48. In Ferguson, *Chasing the Wild Goose*, 25.
49. Ferguson, *Chasing the Wild Goose*, 65.
50. Power, "Place of Community," 43.

workers, worship and work were connected and flowed into one another. Early photographs suggest that the men attended worship in their working clothes.[51] This ethos continues today with pilgrims, resident staff, and visitors invited to come as they are for the twice-daily services in the abbey. Additionally, original liturgies have been developed to recognize the different backgrounds of the worshippers—an extension of the community's commitment to hospitality. Weekly services focus on justice, peace, and healing, and include regular celebration of the eucharist.[52] All services (or at least their basic structures) are contained in the *Iona Abbey Worship Book*, a publication of the community. George MacLeod's understanding that the intersection of the sacred and the secular were part of the "essential grandeur" of reformed worship continues to influence the group's use of contemporary language, music, and the arts in their worship life—both in the abbey and in their published resources.[53] However, the Iona Community has long recognized that while its approach to liturgy and music sustains the community, it is also the community that sustains the music and liturgy.[54]

THE MUSIC OF THE IONA COMMUNITY

The Iona Community views the music and liturgy of their services as an opportunity to extend hospitality to the diverse individuals who travel to Iona. Each element of the service is crafted so as to include individuals who come from varying faith backgrounds or none at all. This includes music. While the Iona Community has contributed a vast number of new hymn texts and tunes to the congregational song repertoire, it is a "musical hospitality" and a commitment to including songs of the other, selections from the global church, and new songs that supplement the traditional forms of church music that ultimately defines their musical identity.[55] The

---

51. Power, "Place of Community," 39.
52. Power, "Place of Community," 39.
53. Hawn, *Gather into One*, 200.
54. Bentley, "Community, Authenticity, Growth," 77.
55. Bentley, "Community, Authenticity, Growth," 71.

community holds that any sense of *communitas* developed amongst the pilgrims must be jointly constructed each time the assembly gathers for worship. This necessitates an approach to musical engagement that makes all feel welcome and includes people of varying skill levels.

Most worship services in the Iona Abbey include a time of musical instruction. It is never assumed that those gathered will be familiar with the music included in the service. Due to this, each song is first taught by the musician using eurythmics and, in many cases, without the aid of printed sheet music. However, this instruction time is not simply about learning new songs; it is also a means by which individuals are invited into the collective group. The music is used to create and reinforce both individual identity and a group dynamic from the beginning of the worship experience.[56] Additionally, great emphasis is placed on the musical integrity of any song used in the service of worship. Care is taken to ensure the appropriateness of a song for the particular worship service, its liturgical function, and its relevancy to the group of pilgrims, current events, and the wider community life. These criteria have led to the inclusion of a great diversity of sung resources, creating the opportunity for liminality through their musical diversity.[57] Similar to the Taizé Community, the Iona Community has discovered over the decades of its communal life that this commitment to the inclusion of all people in the music of their services and the use of diverse music to form community has necessitated the composition of new resources.

The creation of new musical resources for the Iona Community has largely been the work of John L. Bell (b. 1949), Graham Maule (1958–2019), and the members of the Wild Goose Resource Group, a semiautonomous project of the organization.[58] Bell and Maule began their affiliation with the Iona Community as youth workers in the 1980s. The two perceived a lack of music around issues of poverty and diversity, leading them to pen a number of

---

56. Bentley, "Community, Authenticity, Growth," 72–73.
57. Hawn, *Gather into One*, 214.
58. Ferguson, *Chasing the Wild Goose*, 134.

new hymn texts which they set to traditional Scottish folk songs. Quickly, Bell's ability to write poetic words that expressed contemporary issues in evocative ways with exceedingly accessible melodies made the music of the Iona Community and Wild Geese an important resource for the ecumenical church.[59] Bell, a Church of Scotland minister, became the prominent figure promoting the group's extensive song collections, anthems, shorter songs, and liturgies around the world.[60]

Bell's writings and workshops, particularly in his books *The Singing Thing* (2000) and *The Singing Thing Too* (2007), dramatically influenced the worship life and musical approach of the Iona Community. However, he is quick to say that the music and this ethos were established through the communal efforts of the Wild Geese. Bell claims:

> The songs from Iona are not composed in solitude on the beach of the tiny island off the western coast of Scotland with the waves lapping at the shore. [They are] the product of ongoing argument, experiment, study, discussion, questioning, and listening to the conversation of ordinary people.[61]

The "Big Sing," a uniquely Iona term for the weekly hymn practices, and the expressions of the gathered community continue to shape and inform the musical identity of the organization. As Jane Bentley, a community music expert and former Iona staff member, asserts, "music is seen not just as a tool for expression, but also for growth."[62] It is with this in mind that the Iona Community approaches music as a way of shaping the story and beliefs of the gathered assembly. It remains a part of the abbey musician's job to "ensure that music in the services challenges and expands the horizons of participants."[63] The ever-changing pilgrimage group and the Iona Community's commitment to peace and justice, diversity, and

---

59. Hawn, *New Songs of Celebration Render*, 307.
60. Ferguson, *Chasing the Wild Goose*, 134.
61. In Hawn, *Gather into One*, 208.
62. Bentley, "Community, Authenticity, Growth," 75–76.
63. Iona Community Musician's post description, 2019.

singing the song of the other, means that the musical resources of the organization's worship continue to expand and change.

SOCIAL JUSTICE, POLITICS, ADVOCACY, AND THE IONA PILGRIMAGE EXPERIENCE

For the pilgrim visiting Iona, the interconnectedness of justice, politics, worship, and faith is inescapable. George MacLeod asserted that "all life should be sacrament," a charge that continues to inform the life, work, and worship of the community.[64] From the beginning, MacLeod saw Iona as being positioned to impact ecumenical relationships and to shape international justice through personal holiness.[65] The transformation of the individual pilgrim is only realized by their ability to shape discourse in their home communities.

Pilgrims visiting and joining in the common life of the Iona Community may expect to experience worship and music that links together work, prayer, and politics. These central themes bring together the community's commitment to both personal and global healing, peace, and justice.[66] For the Iona Community, prayer is at the heart of radical change. Since the 1940s, this has manifest itself in an advocacy for relevant, contemporary worship around challenging themes, with frequent celebration of the Eucharist—a position that has often put them at odds with church leaders and accepted practice. Additionally, MacLeod's vision for worship was that the responses—spoken and musical—would be reflective of the priesthood of *all* believers and, in all things, focused on justice.[67]

For the Iona Community, justice is central to their purpose for existing. As Ferguson puts it, "justice is at the very heart of the faith, not an optional extra."[68] For pilgrims, this means that worship and the common life must include prayer and work for justice and peace.

64. Hawn, *Gather into One*, 200.
65. Ferguson, *Chasing the Wild Goose*, 93.
66. Ferguson, *Chasing the Wild Goose*, 114.
67. Ferguson, *Chasing the Wild Goose*, 62.
68. Ferguson, *Chasing the Wild Goose*, 149.

The community's desire is that these practices, experienced for only a short time on the island, might influence the lives and work of pilgrims after they have returned home.[69] Through the efforts of the community and the publications of the Wild Goose Resource Group, this message of justice and peace has become embedded in liturgical form. As one former warden of the abbey put it, the hope of the Iona Community is that pilgrims might "arrive seeking peace and quiet but leave seeking peace and justice."[70] The Celtic symbol for the Holy Spirit, the Wild Goose, has been used by the Iona Community throughout its history, because it depicts the turbulent reality of the world while acknowledging the unpredictable presence and work of the Holy Spirit. The connection of this turbulent world to worship and music continues to define the life of the Iona Community and the embodied experience of the modern pilgrim. The Iona Community's approach to the connection between politics, worship, and music links it with other pilgrimage experiences throughout history and demonstrates one example of how pilgrimage and its music might become fixed in liturgical practices in local communities. How this practice might change local congregations' approaches to music and liturgy, as well as the ability of pilgrimage experiences and practices to change political and ecclesiastical structures in a postmodern world, remains for new individuals and communities to discover in the post-COVID world.

---

69. Ferguson, *Chasing the Wild Goose*, 130.
70. In Bentley, "Community, Authenticity, Growth," 72.

5

We'll All Walk Together

*Guidelines and Suggestions for
Pilgrimage in Local Congregations*

*We are pilgrims on a journey;
we're together on the road.
We are here to help each other
walk the mile and bear the load.*[1]

INTRODUCTION TO RESOURCES

As stated throughout, embracing the pilgrimage discipline is an individual and contextual action. Bearing this in mind, any suggested sites of pilgrimage, music, or liturgy are subjective. Churches wishing to engage this discipline more fully should tailor these resources to best reflect their community's understanding, purpose, and need. This is in keeping with pilgrimage's focus on the individual's context of meaning. That which follows are only suggestions.

These suggestions are offered to engage those seeking a deeper understanding of pilgrimage in a conversation about the ways in

---

1. Stanza two of "The Servant Song," Text and music by Richard Gillard © 1977 Universal Music—Brentwood Benson Publishing.

which their practices, both on the journey and at home, can be enhanced through music, liturgy, and discussion. Liturgy means the work of the people. Space is allowed in each of these suggested prayers for the gathered community to engage in reflection, conversation, and musicmaking that is spontaneous to their circumstance and/or created in the moment. The music suggested throughout is that—a suggestion. It may be preferable for some music to repeated along the journey. Group leaders should feel free to repeat songs that are particularly meaningful to the group or add other songs, prayers, or elements to the liturgies that connect to their particular context. It is advised that the songs for the walking liturgy (and others) be learned before the journey. The musical accompaniment should be chosen for that which best suits the group's needs. Some of the songs suggested will require a more skilled song leader and/or accompaniment while others may be performed either a cappella or with a simple guitar accompaniment. Again, the group should make decisions based on what best fits their needs. Additionally, resources are provided for those who remain at home.

For ancient Israel, certain times were set aside for daily worship in the temple, upper rooms, and at home. This practice has continued up to modern times. In monastic communities, daily prayer is essential to building cohesion and establishing routine practices for the group. On pilgrimage, engagement with daily prayer provides a consistent and safe space for pilgrims to engage with one another among the different and changing environments of the journey. Daily prayer provides a structure for the pilgrimage experience, keeping the group focused on their shared discipline. Finally, daily prayer plays a significant role in developing relationships—as discussed in chapter 3.

Most Christian traditions provide a similar understanding of the daily prayer practice.[2] These worship experiences, designed to take place most frequently outside of the church, focus on communal prayer and praise for God. Preaching or extended teaching

---

2. See the United Methodist Church's *Book of Worship*, the Presbyterian Church (USA)'s *Book of Common Worship*, the Evangelical Lutheran Church in America's *Evangelical Lutheran Worship*, among others for simple explanations of daily prayer and samples for other services.

is not a part of the daily prayer practice. The services that follow use a simple pattern of gathering, singing, Scripture, and prayer. Silence is also a useful tool in these experiences and should not be ignored.

The journey of the pilgrim shapes the communities through which they travel and to which they return. The hoped-for transformation of pilgrimage is a wider worldview and a new social reality as a result of the new practices and understandings gained on the journey. To ease this transition for the home community, individuals who stay home are invited to use similar liturgies, music, and reflection to consider how they may be in solidarity with the pilgrimage community.

The following liturgies are offered as models for use on pilgrimage:

1. *A Liturgy for Use before Leaving (page xx)*
2. *A Liturgy at the Airport, Bus, or Van (page xx)*
3. *A Liturgy for Walking (page xx)*
4. *A Liturgy of Arrival and Departure (page xx)*
5. *A Morning Office (page xx)*
6. *A Liturgy before the Meal (page xx)*
7. *Evening Prayer before Bed [Compline] (page xx)*
8. *A Liturgy for Going Home (page xx)*
9. *A Liturgy for the Return (page xx)*

We'll All Walk Together

LITURGIES FOR PILGRIMAGE

1. *A Liturgy for Use before Leaving*

This liturgy is designed to include both individuals embarking on a pilgrimage and those remaining at home. The use of printed materials or projected responses is assumed in this liturgy. The **bold text** indicates those parts spoken by the assembly.

OPENING SENTENCES

O Lord, open our lips.
And our mouths shall proclaim your praise. (Ps 51:15)
How very good it is, how wonderful (Ps 133:1–3, paraphrased)
for God's people to live together in unity.
It is like precious oil poured on the head,
it is like the dew falling gently on the mountains.
How very good it is, how wonderful
for God's people to live together in unity.
Open our lips, O Lord,
and we will worship you, and we will praise you.

The Opening Sentences may also be sung using:
"¡Miren Qué Bueno! (O Look and Wonder)"—**MIREN QUÉ BUENO**[3]

OPENING HYMN

"Guide Me, O Thou Great Jehovah"—**CWM RHONDDA**[4]

---

3. Text and music by Pablo Sosa © 1972 by GIA Publications, Inc. Pablo Sosa's Argentinian hymn is a paraphrase of Psalm 133. It may be performed without the use of printed materials with the assembly singing the refrain/estribillo and a cantor singing the stanzas. See https://hymnary.org/text/how_good_it_is_when_brothers.

4. It may be preferable to use the plural form, "Guide us, O Thou great Jehovah, pilgrims" for this service as in the Society for the Promotion of Christian Knowledge's *Hymns for Public Use* (1852). See Alan Luff, "Guide me, O

PRAYER FOR ILLUMINATION

The grass withers and the flower fades, (Isa 40:8)
but your word, O God, stands forever.
Open our hearts and minds to hear what you are saying to us today.
Amen.

PSALM 121

I lift up my eyes to the hills—
from where will my help come?
My help comes from the Lord,
who made heaven and earth.
He will not let your foot be moved;
he who keeps you will not slumber.
He who keeps Israel
will neither slumber nor sleep.
The Lord is your keeper;
the Lord is your shade at your right hand.
The sun shall not strike you by day,
nor the moon by night.
The Lord will keep you from all evil;
he will keep your life.
The Lord will keep your going out and your coming in
from this time on and forevermore.

HYMN OR SONG *(to be selected from the following)*

"I Will Lift My Eyes to the Mountains"—Tony Alonso[5]
"Total Praise"—Richard Smallwood[6]

Thou Great Jehovah (Redeemer)," *The Canterbury Dictionary of Hymnology*, Canterbury Press, http://www.hymnology.co.uk/g/guide-me,-o-thou-great-jehovah-(redeemer) (accessed 8 January 2021).

    5. Text and Music by Tony Alonso © 2014 by GIA Music Publications, Inc. G-8675.

    6. Text and Music by Richard Smallwood © 1990 Bridge Building Music and T. Autumn Music (admin. CapitolCMGPublishing.

"To the Hills I Lift My Eyes"—**NA-UI DO-UM**[7]
"My Help Comes Only from the Lord (A responsorial setting)"—Daniel Richardson/Angel Napieralski[8]

READING 3 John 1:5–8 (ESV, ed.[9])

[5]Beloved, it is a faithful thing you do in all your efforts for these brothers [and sisters], strangers as they are, [6] who testified to your love before the church. You will do well to send them on their journey in a manner worthy of God. [7]For they have gone out for the sake of [God]. [8]Therefore we ought to support people like these, that we may be fellow [companions on the search] for truth.

REFLECTION

A short reflection may be offered on the biblical characters whose stories began with a journey (i.e. Abram, Jonah, the disciples, Jesus, etc.). The reflection should express a hope for transformation as a result of the journey while acknowledging potential difficulty as a result of the pilgrimage.

If the worship allows, participants should be invited to share their hopes, expectations, and fears before the journey. Individuals staying behind may share similar thoughts.

---

com). Available in the hymnals listed at https://hymnary.org/text/lord_i_will_lift_mine_eyes_to_the_hills.

7. Text: Song-suk Im, 1990, English translation by Emily R. Brink, 2011; Music: Song Lee, 1990.
Text, English translation, and Music © 1990, 2011 by Christian Conference of Asia (admin. GIA Publications, Inc.) See https://hymnary.org/text/to_the_hills_i_lift_my_eyes_longing_to.

8. Music: Daniel Richardson and Angel Napieralski © 2010 admin. Faith Alive Christian Resources. This responsorial psalm setting, included in Witvliet et al., *Psalms for All Seasons,* may be performed without the use of printed materials with the assembly singing the refrain and a cantor singing the verses.

9. Here and elsewhere, "ed." will refer to text which I have edited for non-masculine language.

The reflection should conclude with an acknowledgment of a shared community between those staying behind, those leaving, and those yet to be met along the way.

COMMISSIONING

Throughout history, God has called God's children to different forms of ministry. Today, we acknowledge God's call to each of you to continue your faith journey in a new place and the call to experience the joys and sorrows, hopes and dreams, and transformation that comes with experiencing God in different locations and formed in new relationships with God's people. Travel extends our connection to God's family. So, as we send you forth [*or* as we are sent forth], we ask you the following questions:

To the participants:
Do you receive this call as a gift of the Holy Spirit, and will you rely on the Spirit to support, sustain, challenge, and comfort you along this journey you are taking?

I do, and I will.

Will you be faithful in your participation during this journey, receptive to the experience of new community with those traveling with you and those you will encounter along the way? Will you be attentive to the details of the trip but also open to surprises and the intervention of God's Spirit as you go?

I will with God's help.

Will you return and share the knowledge, insights, wisdom, questions, and imperatives for action you will have gained through this experience with those who stay behind?

I will.

To the congregation:
Will you, the congregation, hold these travelers in prayer and surround them with the love of God in their absence?

We will.

Will you receive these participants *(names may be inserted)* when they return, listen to their stories, open to the spiritual insights they have gained from their journey welcoming them back into the community?

We will.

Let us pray.
Holy God, you are in this place and in all places. We ask your blessing on these individuals *(names may be inserted)* who travel today *(location may be inserted)*. Open their hearts and minds to experience you in new ways as they meet you in those they encounter along the way. May they experience the mystery of the body of Christ which is alive across national boundaries and cultural lines. May they be encouraged, renewed, and transformed by your Holy Spirit, and may those who stay behind be ready to hear their stories, learn from them, and welcome them when they return. We pray in the name of the One who was, and is, and shall be ever more. Amen.

HYMN (to be selected from the following)

"Lord, as We Rise to Leave the Shell of Worship"—**LOBET DEN HERREN**[10]
"In the Midst of New Dimensions"—**NEW DIMENSIONS**[11]

---

10. Text by Fred Kaan © 1968 Hope Publishing Company. See https://hymnary.org/text/lord_as_we_rise_to_leave_the_shell_of_wo.

11. Text and Music © 1994 Julian B. Rush. See https://hymnary.org/text/in_the_midst_of_new_dimensions.

CLOSING SENTENCES

May the God of hope fill us with all joy and peace (Rom 15:13) through the power of the Holy Spirit.
Amen.

> Bless the Lord.
> **The Lord's name be praised.**

DISMISSAL HYMN

"In Christ There Is No East or West"—**MCKEE**[12]

Additional hymn/song options:
"Oh, the Life of the World Is a Joy and a Treasure"—**LIFE OF THE WORLD**[13]
"Walk Together Children"—African American Spiritual[14]
"I to the Hills Will Lift My Eyes"—**DUNDEE**[15]

---

12. Text: John Oxenham, 1908, alt.; Music: African American Spiritual; *Jubilee Songs*, 1884; adapt. Harry T. Burleigh, 1940. See https://hymnary.org/text/in_christ_there_is_no_east_or_west_oxenh.

13. Text and tune © Rev. Kathy Galloway/Iona Community. See the *Iona Abbey Worship Book*.

14. African American Spiritual, Public Domain. This song may be performed without the use of printed materials. See https://hymnary.org/text/walk_together_children_dont_you_get_wear.

15. Text: *The New Metrical Version of the Psalms*, 1909, alt.; Music: Scottish Psalter, 1615. See https://hymnary.org/text/i_to_the_hills_will_lift_mine_eyes_from.

2. A Liturgy at the Airport, Bus, or Van

This liturgy is designed to be used without printed materials to encourage brevity. The **bold text** indicates those parts spoken by the assembly.

OPENING SENTENCES

The Opening Sentences are sung using:
"¡Miren Qué Bueno! (O Look and Wonder)"—**MIREN QUÉ BUENO**[16]

The following may be used in place of the sung Opening Sentences:
The assembly responds to the petition, "How good it is, how wonderful for God's people," saying, **"to live together in unity."**

How good it is, how wonderful for God's people (Ps 133:1)
to live together in unity.
God knows our going out and our coming in. (Ps 121:8)
How good it is, how wonderful for God's people
to live together in unity.
God is our refuge, our home,
and our protector on the way. (Ps 91:9–11)
How good it is, how wonderful for God's people
to live together in unity.
Trusting in God's promises,
let us journey on in worship and prayer.

OPENING HYMN

"We Must Leave Home"—**LUNDY'S LANE**/Shirley Erena Murray[17]

---

16. Text and Music by Pablo Sosa © 1972 by GIA Publications. Pablo Sosa's Argentinian hymn is a paraphrase of Psalm 133. It may be performed without the use of printed materials with the assembly singing the refrain/estribillo and a cantor singing the stanzas.

17. Words and Music © 2013 Hope Publishing Company. See https://www.hopepublishing.com/find-hymns-hw/hw5170.aspx. This largely unknown

From *Plague to Purpose*

PSALM 120 (ESV)

In my distress I called to the Lord,
and he answered me.
Deliver me, O Lord,
from lying lips,
from a deceitful tongue.
What shall be given to you,
and what more shall be done to you,
you deceitful tongue?
A warrior's sharp arrows,
with glowing coals of the broom tree!
Woe to me, that I sojourn in Meshech,
that I dwell among the tents of Kedar!
Too long have I had my dwelling
among those who hate peace.
I am for peace,
but when I speak, they are for war!

READING Genesis 12:1–3 (ESV, ed.)

Now the Lord said to Abram, "Go from your country and your kindred and your father's house to the land that I will show you. ²And I will make of you a great nation, and I will bless you and make your name great, so that you will be a blessing. ³I will bless those who bless you, and in you all the families of the earth shall be blessed."

---

hymn may be performed paperless with the assembly singing the refrain only. While not well known, the text and tune provide a fitting metaphor for embarking on an unknown journey. Pilgrimage leaders should embrace unfamiliar worship resources to connect to the unknown realities of the pilgrimage venture. The more familiar "God of Grace and God of Glory"/CWM RHONDDA would be an acceptable substitution, if necessary.

PRAYERS OF THANKSGIVING AND INTERCESSION

Sojourning God,
You called to Abraham to get up and go.
We give you thanks for the similar calling you have given to each of us.
We pray that, like our forefathers and foremothers, our footsteps might lead us to
a deeper faith and trust in you.
We give you thanks for those that have made our travel possible:
for planners,
for generous financial contributors,
and for those staying behind who support us with their prayers.
We give you thanks for those who will provide for our safety:
for bus drivers, pilots, and guides,
for our hosts and cooks,
and for those whose faithful work sustains our journey out of sight.
We give you thanks for those we are yet to encounter.
We know that "Christ comes in the stranger's guise," and so we pray for your companionship on our journey,
for openness to the experience and, most importantly, to the people whom we will meet.
May we approach each encounter as one with the risen Christ.
Traveling God,
Like Abraham, Moses, Paul, and Jesus,
call us to heed the challenge of pilgrimage.
Call us to step out in faith.
Call us to seek justice, peace, and to walk humbly with you our God.
By this pilgrimage, change us so that we may become better disciples in the days to come.
We pray these things in the name of our incarnate savior, Jesus Christ,
Amen.

SONG

"Spirit, Spirit of Gentleness"—SPIRIT[18]

CLOSING SENTENCES

May the God of hope fill us with all joy and peace (Rom 15:13) through the power of the Holy Spirit.
Amen.

Bless the Lord.
The Lord's name be praised.

DISMISSAL SONG *(to be selected from the following)*

"Now Go in Peace"—JUNKANOO[19]
"Thuma Mina (Send Me, Jesus)"—South Africa[20]

Additional Hymn Option:

"The Summons"—KELVINGROVE[21]

---

18. Text and Music © 1978 James K. Manley. To perform without the use of printed materials, the assembly should sing the refrain with a cantor/soloist singing the stanzas. See https://hymnary.org/text/you_moved_on_the_waters.

19. Text: Michael Mair © Church of Scotland Panel on Worship; Music: Caribbean folk melody. This song may be performed as a canon without the use of printed materials. See *Church Hymnary IV*.

20. Text and Music in *Freedom is Coming* © 1984 Walton Music Corp. This song may be performed without the use of printed materials. See https://hymnary.org/text/thuma_mina_thuma_mina.

21. Text: John L. Bell and Graham Maule; Music: Scottish melody; arr. John L. Bell © 1987 WGRG, Iona Community (admin. GIA Publications, Inc.). See https://hymnary.org/text/will_you_come_and_follow_me.

3. A Liturgy for Walking

This liturgy is designed to be used without printed materials as people are walking. The **bold text** indicates those parts spoken by the assembly. Spoken responses are kept to a minimum. Multiple voices may be used in the Scripture collage with individuals memorizing their individual lines and offering them in any order. Additionally, a sung refrain may be inserted in between each section. To be most effective, the songs should be learned prior to departure.

OPENING SONG(S)

"Sarantanani (Let's Walk Together)"—Bolivia[22]
"Jikelele (Walk with Jesus around the World)"—South Africa[23]
"Ewe Thina (We Walk His Way)"—South Africa[24]

OPENING SENTENCES/SCRIPTURE COLLAGE

The assembly responds to the statement, "Happy are those who obey the Lord" replying, **"who walk in God's ways."**

To you I lift up my eyes,
O you who are enthroned in the heavens! (Ps 123:1)
Happy are those who obey the Lord,
who walk in God's ways.

---

22. Text translated by John L. Bell; Music: Bolivian folk melody © 2008 WGRG, Iona Community (admin. GIA Publications, Inc.). This song may be performed without the use of printed materials. See Bell and Adam, *Sing the World*, GIA Publications G-7339.

23. Text translated by John L. Bell; Music: Zulu/South African © 2012 WGRG, Iona Community (admin. GIA Publications, Inc.). This song may be performed without the use of printed materials. See: Bell, *Truth That Sets Us Free*, GIA Publications G-8503.

24. Text translated by John L. Bell; Music: South Africa © 2008 WGRG, Iona Community (admin. GIA Publications, Inc.). This song may be performed without the use of printed materials. See Bell, *We Walk His Way*, GIA Publications G-7403.

Our eyes look to the Lord our God,
who has mercy upon us. (Ps 123:2b)
Happy are those who obey the Lord,
who walk in God's ways.

Those who trust in the Lord are like Mount Zion,
which cannot be moved, but abides forever. (Ps 125:1)
Happy are those who obey the Lord,
who walk in God's ways.

As the mountains surround Jerusalem,
so the Lord surrounds his people. (Ps 125:2)
Happy are those who obey the Lord,
who walk in God's ways.

Do good, O Lord, to those who are good,
and to those who are upright in their hearts. (Ps 125:4)
Happy are those who obey the Lord,
who walk in God's ways.

Happy is everyone who fears the Lord,
who walks in his ways.
You shall eat the fruit of the labor of your hands;
you shall be happy, and it shall go well with you. (Ps 128:1–2)
Happy are those who obey the Lord,
who walk in God's ways.

SONG/HYMN(S)

"I Want Jesus to Walk with Me"—African-American Spiritual[25]
"Leaning on the Everlasting Arms"—**SHOWALTER**[26]

---

25. African American Spiritual, Public Domain. Ideally, this song may be performed without the use of printed materials. See https://hymnary.org/text/i_want_jesus_to_walk_with_me.

26. Text: Elisha A. Hoffman, 1887; Anthony J. Showalter, 1887, Public Domain. Ideally, this song may be performed without the use of printed materials. See https://hymnary.org/text/what_a_fellowship_what_a_joy_divine.

We'll All Walk Together

READING Proverbs 3:1–2, 5–8, 13–14, 21–27 (ESV)

My child, do not forget my teaching,
but let your heart keep my commandments;
for length of days and years of life
and abundant welfare they will give you.

Song

Trust in the Lord with all your heart,
and do not rely on your own insight.
In all your ways acknowledge him,
and he will make straight your paths.
Do not be wise in your own eyes;
fear the Lord and turn away from evil.
It will be a healing for your flesh
and a refreshment for your body.

Song

Happy are those who find wisdom,
and those who get understanding,
for her income is better than silver,
and her revenue better than gold.

Song

My child, do not let these escape from your sight:
keep sound wisdom and prudence,
and they will be life for your soul
and adornment for your neck.
Then you will walk on your way securely
and your foot will not stumble.
If you sit down, you will not be afraid;
when you lie down, your sleep will be sweet.
Do not be afraid of sudden panic,
or of the storm that strikes the wicked;

for the Lord will be your confidence
and will keep your foot from being caught.

Song

Suggested songs to accompany the reading:
"Sizohamba Naye (We Will Walk with God, My Brothers)"—Swaziland[27]
"Siyahamba (We Are Marching in the Light of God)"—South Africa[28]

PRAYER & THE LORD'S PRAYER

The assembly responds to the petition, "God, in your mercy," replying, **"hear our prayer."**

God, we pray for your creation,
for the mountains, oceans, and sky,
and for animals great and small.
Make us more mindful of our interconnectedness
and our shared responsibility to care for your creation.

God, in your mercy,
hear our prayer.

We pray for communities around the world,
for those we are a part of, those through which we travel,
and those that we may never know.

27. Text: Swaziland, translated by John L. Bell, 2002; Music: Swaziland Melody, arr. John L. Bell, 2008 © 2008 WGRG, Iona Community (admin. GIA Publications, Inc.). This song may be performed without the use of printed materials. The song leader should feel empowered to add additional lyrics, as able. See https://hymnary.org/text/we_will_walk_with_god_my_brothers.

28. Text: South African, translated by Gracia Grindal, 1984; Music: South African, arr. *Freedom is Coming*, 1984 © 1984 Utryck (admin. Walton Music Corporation). This song may be performed without the use of printed materials. The song leader should feel empowered to add additional lyrics, as able. See https://hymnary.org/text/we_are_marching_in_the_light_of_god.

Help us to understand our collective humanity
that we might rise above our individual interests.
God, in your mercy,
hear our prayer.

We pray for fellow sojourners.
May we each discover the divine in the places of our wanderings.
May we be changed to become better vessels of your peace
and agents of justice and reconciliation.
God, in your mercy,
hear our prayer.

Finally, we pray for ourselves.
Be our companion on our journey.
Give us wisdom, guard our ways,
and help us to not fear the new future to which you call us.
God, in your mercy,
hear our prayer.

Almighty God, maker of heaven and earth,
be with us in our journeying,
that we might follow you always.
We pray all this in the name of the one who went before us and
taught us to pray together. . .

Participants should be encouraged to pray the Lord's Prayer in their own native tongue and the version with which they are most comfortable.

CLOSING SONG(S)

"Walk in Peace"—**WALKING PIECE**/Adam Tice[29]
"Guide My Feet"—African American Spiritual[30]

29. Included in the collection *Stars Like Grace* (Chicago: GIA Music Publications, 2013). This song may be performed without the use of printed materials.

30. African American Spiritual, Public Domain. This song may be

4. A Liturgy of Arrival and Departure

This liturgy may use printed materials or be conducted paperless. The songs indicated with an asterisk (*) denote those most suitable for use without printed materials. When possible, multiple voices should be utilized to lead various portions of the service. The **bold text** indicates those parts spoken by the assembly. The brackets [] indicate a shorter reading, if desired.

OPENING SONG(S)

"Come into His Presence Singing Alleluia"—COME INTO HIS PRESENCE*[31]
"Come, Ye That Love the Lord"—MARCHING TO ZION[32]
"Brethren, We Have Met to Worship"—HOLY MANNA[33]

OPENING SENTENCES (Ps 122:1–2, 6–9, ed.)

I was glad when they said to me,
"Let us go to the house of the Lord!"
Our feet are standing within your gates, O Jerusalem.
To it the tribes of the Lord go up,
to give thanks to the name of the Lord.
Pray for the peace of Jerusalem:
"May they prosper who love you.
Peace be within your walls."
For the sake of my relatives and friends
I will say, "Peace be within you."

---

performed without the use of printed materials. See https://hymnary.org/text/guide_my_feet_while_i_run_this_race.

31. Text and Music: Anonymous, Public Domain. This song may also be performed as a canon. See https://hymnary.org/text/come_into_his_presence_singing_alleluia.

32. Text: Isaac Watts; Music: Robert Lowry, Public Domain. See https://hymnary.org/text/come_we_that_love_the_lord_and_let_our.

33. Text: George Askins, 1817; Music: *Columbian Harmony*: 1825, Public Domain. See https://hymnary.org/text/brethren_we_have_met_to_worship.

**For the sake of the house of the Lord our God,
I will seek your good.**

OPENING HYMN/SONG *(to be selected from the following)*

"I Rejoiced When I Heard Them Say"—**ENGLAND***[34]
"Gather Us In"—Marty Haugen[35]
"Praise to the Lord, the Almighty"—**LOBE DEN HERREN**[36]

READINGS Revelation 21:1–7 (ESV)

[Then I saw a new heaven and a new earth, for the first heaven and the first earth had passed away, and the sea was no more. ²And I saw the holy city, new Jerusalem, coming down out of heaven from God, prepared as a bride adorned for her husband. ³And I heard a loud voice from the throne saying, "Behold, the dwelling place of God is with man. He will dwell with them, and they will be his people, and God himself will be with them as their God.] ⁴He will wipe away every tear from their eyes, and death shall be no more, neither shall there be mourning, nor crying, nor pain anymore, for the former things have passed away."

⁵And he who was seated on the throne said, "Behold, I am making all things new." Also he said, "Write this down, for these words are trustworthy and true." ⁶And he said to me, "It is done! I am the Alpha and the Omega, the beginning and the end. To the thirsty I will give from the spring of the water of life without payment. ⁷The one who conquers will have this heritage, and I will be his God and he will be my son."

---

34. Text and Music © 1993 Bernadette Farrell (Published by OCP). This song may be performed without the use of printed materials with the assembly singing only the refrain. See https://hymnary.org/text/i_rejoiced_when_i_heard_them_say_farrell.

35. Text and Music © 1982 GIA Publications, Inc. See https://hymnary.org/text/here_in_this_place_new_light_is_stream.

36. Text: Joachim Neander, 1680, translated by Catherine Winkworth, 1863; Music: Stralsund *Ernewerten Gesangbuch,* 1665, Public Domain. See https://hymnary.org/text/praise_to_the_lord_the_almighty_the_king.

From *Plague to Purpose*

2 Corinthians 3:18

And we all, with unveiled face, beholding the glory of the Lord, are being transformed into the same image from one degree of glory to another. For this comes from the Lord who is the Spirit.

LITANY OF THANKSGIVING

Merciful God,
you were with those who traveled before us, with Moses and Miriam, Mary and Joseph, Paul and Silas.
So, we give you thanks for our safe journey to this destination.
We recognize that our arrival does not mark an ending
but a new beginning,
and so, we offer our voices in praise.

Song

Loving God,
you met the disciples on the road.
So, we give you thanks for those we have encountered on the way,
for unexpected blessings, deeper relationships,
and opportunities to meet you in the mundane and the surreal.
We offer our voices in praise.

Song

Creating God,
you promised that you are making all things new.
So, we give you thanks that our pilgrimage is not over,
rather that the journey and this arrival mark a transformation in us.
You call us to greater discipleship and to deeper faith.
May this journey enable that growth
as we offer our voices in praise.

Song

Suffering God,
on the cross, you stood in solidarity with all of humanity.
So, we give you thanks for the ways our journey has opened our eyes
to injustice, different cultures, and new understandings.
You call us to do justice, to love kindness,
and to walk humbly with you.
May this journey enliven a deep desire within us to do just that.
We offer our voices in praise.

Song

Sustaining God,
you promised us the gift of the Holy Spirit to guide us.
So, we give you thanks for the ways
in which your Spirit is moving in each of us
renewing, redeeming, and reshaping us for your kingdom.
You call us to be the salt of the earth and light for the world,
may our departure from this place be only the beginning.
In gratitude and anticipation, we offer our voices in praise.

Song

Suggested songs to accompany the litany:
"Behold, I Make All Things New"—John L. Bell*[37]
"Breathe on Me, Breath of God"—**TRENTHAM**[38]

COMMUNION (optional)

If desired, the Eucharist may be celebrated at this point in the service. Leaders should adapt a communion liturgy from their own tradition for use. If no ordained person is traveling on the pilgrimage, groups are encouraged to explore the Love Feast/Agape meal in their tradition.

---

37. In *Come All You People: Shorter Songs for Worship* by John L. Bell © 1994, WGRG (admin. GIA Publications, Inc.) G-4391.

38. Text: Edwin Hatch, 1878; Music: Robert Jackson, 1888, Public Domain. See https://hymnary.org/text/breathe_on_me_breath_of_god.

Suggested hymn(s) to accompany the celebration of communion:
"This Is a Day of New Beginnings"—**BEGINNINGS**[39]
"Amazing Grace! (How Sweet the Sound)"—**AMAZING GRACE**[40]

CLOSING PRAYER

Holy God, you are in this place and in all places. We ask your continued blessing as we travel on today. You have opened our hearts and minds. May our experience of the new ways we meet you continue well beyond this moment. May we continue to experience the mystery of the body of Christ which is alive across all boundaries and cultural lines. May we continue to be encouraged, renewed, and transformed by your Holy Spirit, ever ready to share our stories and to work for transformation and reconciliation in your world. We pray in the name of the One who was, and is, and shall be ever more. Amen.

DISMISSAL HYMNS/SONG(S)

"Wa Wa Wa Emimimo (Come, O Holy Spirit)"—Nigeria*[41]
"Spirit of the Living God"—Daniel Iverson[42]
"Come, Holy Ghost, Our Souls Inspire"—**VENI CREATOR SPIRITUS**[43]

---

39. Text: Brian Wren, 1978, alt. 1987; Music: Carlton R. Young, 1984 © 1987 Hope Publishing Company. See https://www.hopepublishing.com/find-hymns-hw/hw2386.aspx.

40. Text: John Newton, 1779, Public Domain. See https://hymnary.org/text/amazing_grace_how_sweet_the_sound.

41. Text: Nigerian Song, English translation by I-to Loh, 1986; Music: Nigerian melody, taught by Samuel Solanke, transcribed by I-to Loh, 1986 © 1995 General Board of Global Ministries t/a GBGMusik. See https://hymnary.org/text/come_o_holy_spirit_come_holy_spirit.

42. Text and Music © 1935 Birdwing Music (admin. EMICMGPublishing.com). See https://hymnary.org/text/spirit_of_the_living_god_fall_iverson.

43. Text: attributed to Rabanus Maurus, 9th Century, translated by John Cosin, 1627; Music: Plainsong, Mode VIII, Public Domain. See https://

Additional hymn/song suggestions:

"Love Divine, All Loves Excelling"—Various Tunes[44]
"Soon and very Soon"—Andraé Crouch[45]

---

hymnary.org/text/come_holy_ghost_our_souls_inspire.

44. Text: Charles Wesley, 1747, Public Domain. See https://hymnary.org/text/love_divine_all_love_excelling_joy_of_he.

45. Text and Music © 1976 Crouch Music and Bud John Songs (admin. EMICMGPublishing.com). See https://hymnary.org/text/soon_and_very_soon_we_are_going.

5. A Morning Office

This liturgy may use printed materials or be conducted paperless. The songs indicated with an asterisk (*) denote those most suitable for use without printed materials. When possible, multiple voices should be utilized to lead various portions of the service. The **bold text** indicates those parts spoken by the assembly. This liturgy is designed for daily use on pilgrimage. The psalms and/or readings may be changed to reflect the activities of the day. The brackets [] indicate a shorter reading, if desired.

OPENING SENTENCES

O Lord, open our lips.
And our mouths shall proclaim your praise. (Ps 51:15)
How very good it is, how wonderful (Ps 133:1–3, paraphrased)
for God's people to live together in unity.
It is like precious oil poured on the head,
it is like the dew falling gently on the mountains.
How very good it is, how wonderful
for God's people to live together in unity.
Open our lips, O Lord,
and we will worship you,
and we will praise you.

The Opening Sentences may also be sung using:
"¡Miren Qué Bueno! (O Look and Wonder)"—**MIREN QUÉ BUENO**[46]

---

46. Text and Music by Pablo Sosa © 1972 by GIA Music Publications. Pablo Sosa's Argentinian hymn is a paraphrase of Psalm 133. It may be performed without the use of printed materials with the assembly singing the refrain/estribillo and a cantor singing the stanzas.

WE'LL ALL WALK TOGETHER

OPENING HYMN/SONG *(to be selected from the following)*

"Today I Awake"—**SLITHERS OF GOLD**[47]
"Dios Está Aquí (God Is Here Today)"—Raúl Galeano*[48]
"Morning Has Broken"—**BUNESSAN**[49]

OPENING PRAYER

Creator God,
Today is a new day, full of new possibilities.
So, we give you thanks for the gift of the day.
Open our hearts and minds to the experiences you will bring us:
those we anticipate and those beyond our imagination.
Trusting in your goodness and mercy,
we offer our lives to your will this day.
Guide us, lead us, and strengthen us for your work.
We pray in the name of the one who was there in the beginning,
Jesus Christ.
Amen.

PSALM 121 *(or other Psalm of Ascent appropriate for the day)*

I lift up my eyes to the hills—
from where will my help come?
My help comes from the Lord,
who made heaven and earth.
He will not let your foot be moved;
he who keeps you will not slumber.

---

[47]. Text: John L. Bell and Graham Maule; Music: John L. Bell © 1989 WGRG, Iona Community (admin. GIA Publications, Inc.). See https://hymnary.org/text/today_i_awake_and_god_is_before_me.

[48]. Text: Raúl Galeano, 1976 translated by C. Michael Hawn, 1998; Music: Raúl Galeano, 1976 transcribed by C. Michael Hawn and Arturo Gonzalez, 1999 © 1999 Choristers Guild. See https://hymnary.org/text/god_is_here_today_hawn.

[49]. Text: Eleanor Farjeon, 1931; Music: Gaelic Melody, Public Domain. See https://hymnary.org/text/morning_has_broken.

**He who keeps Israel
will neither slumber nor sleep.**
The Lord is your keeper;
the Lord is your shade at your right hand.
**The sun shall not strike you by day,
nor the moon by night.**
The Lord will keep you from all evil;
he will keep your life.
**The Lord will keep your going out and your coming in
from this time on and forevermore.**
(The psalm may also be sung. See additional suggestions for "A Liturgy for Use before Leaving" for appropriate settings of Psalm 121.)

READINGS Genesis 1:1–4 (ESV)

In the beginning, God created the heavens and the earth. ²The earth was without form and void, and darkness was over the face of the deep. And the Spirit of God was hovering over the face of the waters.

³And God said, "Let there be light," and there was light. ⁴And God saw that the light was good. And God separated the light from the darkness.

John 1:1–13 (ESV)

[In the beginning was the Word, and the Word was with God, and the Word was God. ²He was in the beginning with God. ³All things were made through him, and without him was not any thing made that was made. ⁴In him was life, and the life was the light of men. ⁵The light shines in the darkness, and the darkness has not overcome it.]

⁶There was a man sent from God, whose name was John. ⁷He came as a witness, to bear witness about the light, that all might believe through him. ⁸He was not the light, but came to bear witness about the light.

⁹The true light, which gives light to everyone, was coming into the world. ¹⁰He was in the world, and the world was made through

him, yet the world did not know him. ¹¹He came to his own, and his own people did not receive him. ¹²But to all who did receive him, who believed in his name, he gave the right to become children of God, ¹³who were born, not of blood nor of the will of the flesh nor of the will of man, but of God.

PRAYERS OF THANKSGIVING & INTERCESSION

Prayers of thanksgiving and intercession may be extemporaneous and relate to the plans of the day or experiences from the day before. The prayer in "A Liturgy for Walking" may serve as a rough outline for intercessory prayer.

CLOSING SONG/HYMN *(to be selected from the following)*

"I Want to Walk as a Child of the Light"—**HOUSTON**[50]
"Heaven Is Singing for Joy (El Cielo Canta Alegría)"—**ALEGRÍA**[*51]
"I Owe My Lord a Morning Song"—**NAFZIGER**[52]
"I Sing th' Almighty Power of God"—**ELLACOMBE**[53]

This service does not have a benediction as worship continues with the events of the day.

---

50. Text and Music by Kathleen Thomerson, 1966 © 1970, 1975 *Celebration*. See https://hymnary.org/text/i_want_to_walk_as_a_child_of_the_light.

51. Text and Music by Pablo Sosa, 1958 © GIA Publications, Inc. This song may be performed without the use of printed materials with the assembly singing only the refrain. See https://hymnary.org/text/heaven_is_singing_for_joy.

52. Text and Music by John L. Bell © 2000 WGRG, Iona Community (admin. GIA Publications, Inc.). See https://hymnary.org/text/i_owe_my_lord_a_morning_song.

53. Text: Isaac Watts, 1715; Music: *Gesangbuch der Herzogl. Wirtembergischen Katholischen Hofkapelle*, 1784, alt. 1868, Public Domain. See https://hymnary.org/text/i_sing_the_mighty_power_of_god.

6. A Liturgy Before the Meal

This liturgy is designed to be used without printed materials. The **bold text** indicates those parts spoken by the assembly. Spoken responses are kept to a minimum. It is recommended that a different person leads this liturgy each day on the journey. This liturgy borrows from the mealtime practices of the Iona Community.

GATHERING

The beginning of the meal may be signaled with a bell.

OPENING SENTENCES

God is good
All the time.
All the time.
God is good.

(The pilgrimage group may wish to substitute some familiar response from their home community.)

BLESSING

A blessing is offered over the meal, including the hands that picked, prepared, or otherwise made the meal available.

The blessing may also be sung. Some suggestions include:

"God Bless to Us Our Bread (Bendice, Señor, Nuestro Pan)"—Argentina[54]
"For Health and Strength"—**GRACE**[55]

---

54. Collected by Federico Pagura, translated by John L. Bell © 2005 WGRG, Iona Community (admin. GIA Publications, Inc.) See: https://hymnary.org/text/god_bless_to_us_our_bread.

55. Traditional, © J. Curwen and Sons. (admin. ECS Publishing) See:

DISMISSAL

The end of the meal may be signaled with a bell. The host of the meal shares any notices or other information necessary for the rest of the day.

The meal closes with a moment of silence with the leader saying: "Thank you, God" *and the assembly replying,* "**Amen.**"

---

https://hymnary.org/text/for_health_and_strength_and_daily_food.

7. Evening Prayer before Bed [Compline]

This liturgy assumes the use of printed materials. However, the songs indicated with an asterisk (*) denote those most suitable for use without printed materials. When possible, multiple voices should be utilized to lead various portions of the service. The **bold text** indicates those parts spoken by the assembly. This liturgy is designed for daily use on pilgrimage. The psalms and/or readings may be changed to reflect the activities of the day.

OPENING SONG(S)

"Come and Fill"—**CONFITEMINI DOMINO***[56]
"Wait for the Lord"—**WAIT FOR THE LORD***[57]
"Be Still and Know That I Am God"—**PSALM 46***[58]

OPENING SENTENCES (Ps 134)

Come, bless the Lord, all you servants of the Lord,
who stand by night in the house of the Lord!
Lift up your hands to the holy place
and bless the Lord!
May the Lord bless you from Zion,
he who made heaven and earth!

---

56. Text and Music by Jacques Berthier, 1982 © 1991 Les Presses de Taizé (admin. GIA Publications, Inc.). See https://hymnary.org/text/come_and_fill_our_hearts_with_your_peace.

57. Text: Ref. Taizé Community, 1984; Music: Jacques Berthier, 1984 © 1984 Les Presses de Taizé (admin. GIA Publications, Inc.). See https://hymnary.org/text/wait_for_the_lord_whose_day_is_near.

58. Text and Music by John L. Bell, 1989 © 1989 WGRG, Iona Community (admin. GIA Publications, Inc.). See https://hymnary.org/text/be_still_and_know_that_i_am_god_bell.

HYMN/SONG *(to be selected from the following)*

"Lord of All Hopefulness"—**COURTNEY/SLANE**[59]
"For You, My God, I Wait"—**SPRINGTIME**[60]

THANKSGIVING FOR LIGHT

The Lord be with you.
And also with you.
Let us give thanks to the Lord our God.
It is right to give our thanks and praise.

God of God, Light of lights,
we give you thanks for your steadfast love
through this day and all of our days.
We know that darkness is nothing you cannot overcome;
night is only the beginning.
Bless us and keep us this night, O God.
Hold us gently in the palm of your hand
and lead us ever on your way;
we pray through Jesus Christ our Lord,
in fellowship with the Holy Spirit
one God, now and forever.
Amen.

READINGS Genesis 1:1–4 (ESV)

In the beginning, God created the heavens and the earth. ²The earth was without form and void, and darkness was over the face of the deep. And the Spirit of God was hovering over the face of the waters.

---

59. Text: Jan Struther, 1931 © 1931 Oxford University Press; Music: David Schwoebel, 2008 © 2008 Celebrating Grace, Inc. See https://hymnary.org/text/lord_of_all_hopefulness_lord_of_all_joy.

60. Text: Adam M. L. Tice, 2003 © 2011 GIA Publications, Inc.; Music: © 2011 David Ward (admin. Faith Alive Christian Resources). See https://hymnary.org/text/for_you_my_god_i_wait.

³And God said, "Let there be light," and there was light. ⁴And God saw that the light was good. And God separated the light from the darkness.

Mark 13:28–31 (ESV)

"From the fig tree learn its lesson: as soon as its branch becomes tender and puts out its leaves, you know that summer is near. ²⁹So also, when you see these things taking place, you know that he is near, at the very gates. ³⁰Truly, I say to you, this generation will not pass away until all these things take place. ³¹Heaven and earth will pass away, but my words will not pass away."

HYMN *(to be selected from the following)*

"Christ Has Risen"—SUO GAN/HOLY MANNA[61]
"Precious Lord, Take My Hand"—PRECIOUS LORD[62]

PRAYERS OF INTERCESSION & THE LORD'S PRAYER

Prayers of intercession may be extemporaneous and relate to the events of the day or other experiences on the journey. The prayer in "A Liturgy for Walking" may serve as a rough outline for intercessory prayer.

At least a couple of evenings, the prayers should be conducted in a circle, allowing each participant to offer their own prayers or reflections.

Participants should be encouraged to pray the Lord's Prayer in their own native tongue and the version with which they are most comfortable.

---

61. Text: John L. Bell and Graham Maule © 1988 WGRG, Iona Community (admin. GIA Publications, Inc.); Music: Welsh Melody. See https://hymnary.org/text/christ_has_risen_while_earth_slumbers.

62. Text: Thomas A. Dorsey, 1938; Music: George N. Allen, 1844, arr. Thomas A. Dorsey, 1938; Text and Music arrangement © 1938, ren. Warner-Tamerland Publishing Corp. (admin. Alfred Publishing Co., Inc.). See https://hymnary.org/text/precious_lord_take_my_hand.

CLOSING HYMN/SONG *(to be selected from the following)*

"There Is a Longing"—**LONGING**[63]
"We Cannot Measure How You Heal"—**YE BANKS AND BRAES**[64]

CLOSING SENTENCES

May the grace of our Lord Jesus Christ
be with your spirit. (Gal 6:18)
Amen.

Bless the Lord.
The Lord's name be praised.

A sign of peace may be exchanged by all.

---

63. Text and Music © 1992 Anne Quigley (Published by OCP). See https://hymnary.org/text/for_justice_for_freedom_for_mercy.

64. Text: John L. Bell and Graham Maule, 1989; Music: Scottish Melody © 1989 WGRG, Iona Community (admin. GIA Publications, Inc.). See https://hymnary.org/text/we_cannot_measure_how_you_heal.

8. A Liturgy for Going Home

This liturgy assumes the use of printed materials. However, the songs indicated with an asterisk (*) denote those most suitable for use without printed materials, if desired. When possible, multiple voices should be utilized to lead various portions of the service. The **bold text** indicates those parts spoken by the assembly. The brackets [] indicate a shorter reading, if desired.

OPENING SONG *(optional)*

"Sing, Praise, and Bless the Lord"—**LAUDATE DOMINUM (TAIZÉ)***[65]

OPENING SENTENCES (Ps 131, paraphrased)

O Lord, our hearts are not lifted up,
nor are our eyes raised too high;
We do not occupy ourselves with things
too great and too marvelous.
Because our souls have been calmed and quieted,
our hope is in the Lord
from this time on and forevermore.

HYMN *(to be selected from the following)*

"Lord God, Your Love Has Called Us Here"—**RYBURN**[66]
"Restore in Us, O God"—**BAYLOR**[67]

---

[65]. Text: Taizé Community, 1980; Music: Jacques Berthier, 1980; © 1991 Les Presses de Taizé (admin. GIA Publications, Inc.). See https://hymnary.org/text/praise_the_lord_all_you_nations_praise.

[66]. Text: Brian A. Wren © 1977, rev. 1995 Hope Publishing Company; Music: Norman Cocker, Public Domain. See https://hymnary.org/text/great_god_your_love_has_called_us_here.

[67]. Text: Carl P. Daw Jr., 1987 © 1989 Hope Publishing Company; Music: Hal H. Hopson © 1985 Hope Publishing Company. See https://hymnary.org/text/restore_in_us_o_god.

PSALM 127 (ESV)

Unless the Lord builds the house,
those who build it labor in vain.
Unless the Lord watches over the city,
the watchman stays awake in vain.

**It is in vain that you rise up early
and go late to rest,
eating the bread of anxious toil;
for he gives to his beloved sleep.**

Behold, children are a heritage from the Lord,
the fruit of the womb a reward.
Like arrows in the hand of a warrior
are the children of one's youth.

**Blessed is the man
who fills his quiver with them!
He shall not be put to shame
when he speaks with his enemies in the gate.**

READING Jeremiah 29:10-14 (ESV)

"For thus says the Lord: When seventy years are completed for Babylon, I will visit you, and I will fulfill to you my promise and bring you back to this place. [11For I know the plans I have for you, declares the Lord, plans for welfare and not for evil, to give you a future and a hope. 12Then you will call upon me and come and pray to me, and I will hear you. 13You will seek me and find me, when you seek me with all your heart.] 14I will be found by you, declares the Lord, and I will restore your fortunes and gather you from all the nations and all the places where I have driven you, declares the Lord, and I will bring you back to the place from which I sent you into exile.

REFLECTION & SYMBOLIC ACTION

A time of reflection should be offered during this liturgy. Individual participants should be invited to share their experiences and stories as a result of the pilgrimage discipline. These reflections may also include calls to action upon return. This time may also be used to plan post-travel events to share the stories of participants with the local faith community.

It may also be desirable to perform a symbolic action as a part of this reflection time. This may include preparing gifts to leave with hosts or others encountered on the journey. This may also be something as simple as placing a rock in a significant place, signing names in a guest registry, etc. Incorporating such actions in the worship experience codifies them for the entire group.

HYMN *(to be selected from the following)*

"God Is Working His Purpose Out"—**PURPOSE**[68]
"Amazing Grace! (How Sweet the Sound"—**AMAZING GRACE**[69]

PRAYER FOR TRAVEL

God, our refuge and our strength,
we give you thanks and praise for the experiences you have given us through our shared pilgrimage.
We now pray for safe travel as we leave this place,
ready to return to our home communities.
Bless us and keep us safe as we journey on.
We know our journey is never complete until we rest in you.
Until then, Jesus, lead on.
Amen.

---

[68]. Text: Arthur Campbell Ainger, 1894, Public Domain. Other hymns concerned with the call to discipleship may also be substituted in this spot. See https://hymnary.org/text/god_is_working_his_purpose_out.

[69]. Text: John Newton, 1779, Public Domain. See https://hymnary.org/text/amazing_grace_how_sweet_the_sound.

We'll All Walk Together

DISMISSAL HYMN *(to be selected from the following)*

"To God Be the Glory"—**TO GOD BE THE GLORY**[70]
"Great Is Thy Faithfulness"—**FAITHFULNESS**[71]

---

70. Text: Fanny Jane Crosby, 1875; Music: William Howard Doane, 1875, Public Domain. See https://hymnary.org/text/to_god_be_the_glory_great_things_he_hath.

71. Text: Thomas O. Chisholm, 1923; Music: William Marion Runyan, 1923 © 1923, ren. 1951 Hope Publishing Company. See https://hymnary.org/text/great_is_thy_faithfulness_o_god_my_fathe.

FROM *PLAGUE* TO *PURPOSE*

9. A Liturgy for the Return

This liturgy is designed to include both individuals who traveled on a pilgrimage and those who remained at home. The use of printed materials or projected responses is assumed in this liturgy. However, the songs indicated with an asterisk (*) denote those most suitable for use without printed materials, if desired. Additionally, it may be desirable to use songs learned on pilgrimage or shared during the journey in place of those suggested. The **bold text** indicates those parts spoken by the assembly. The brackets [ ] indicate a shorter reading, if desired.

OPENING SONG(S)

"Singing, We Gladly Worship the Lord Together"—**GUATEMALA***[72]
"Live in Charity"—**UBI CARITAS (TAIZÉ)***[73]

OPENING SENTENCES[74] (Ps 126, paraphrased)

Leader: When the Lord restored the fortunes of Zion,
Group A: **we were those who dreamed.**
Our mouths were filled with laughter,
and our tongues with shouts of joy;
then they said among the nations,
Group B: **"The Lord has done great things for them."**
Group A: **The Lord has done great things for us;**
All: **we are glad.**
Leader: Restore our fortunes, O Lord,

---

72. Text: Guatemalan Traditional translated by Christine Caron and John L. Bell; Music: Guatemalan melody © 2005 Christine Carson and WGRG, Iona Community (admin. GIA Publications, Inc.). See https://hymnary.org/text/singing_we_glady_worship_the_lord_togeth.

73. Text: Latin, 8th cent. English translation Taizé Community, 1991; Music: Jacques Berthier, 1979; © 1979 Les Presses de Taizé (admin. GIA Publications, Inc.). See https://hymnary.org/text/ubi_caritas_et_amor.

74. Group A denotes those who traveled, Group B denotes those who stayed home.

Group A: **Let us all celebrate with shouts of joy!**
Leader: Those who went out
Group B: **are welcomed home with shouts of joy,**
All: **Thanks be to God!**

HYMN/SONG *(to be selected from the following)*

"All Are Welcome"—Marty Haugen[75]
"In Christ There Is No East or West"—**MCKEE**[76]
"Take This Moment, Sign, and Space"—John L. Bell[77]

PRAYER FOR ILLUMINATION

The grass withers and the flower fades, (Isa 40:8)
but your word, O God, stands forever.
Open our hearts and minds to hear what you are saying to us today.
Amen.

PSALM 127 (ESV)

Unless the Lord builds the house,
those who build it labor in vain.
Unless the Lord watches over the city,
the watchman stays awake in vain.
It is in vain that you rise up early
and go late to rest,
eating the bread of anxious toil;
for he gives to his beloved sleep.

---

75. Text and Music by Marty Haugen © 1994 GIA Publications, Inc. See https://hymnary.org/text/let_us_build_a_house_where_love_can_dwe.

76. Text: John Oxenham, 1908, alt.; Music: African American Spiritual; *Jubilee Songs,* 1884; adapt. Harry T. Burleigh, 1940. See https://hymnary.org/text/in_christ_there_is_no_east_or_west_oxenh.

77. Text and Music by John L. Bell © 1989 WGRG, Iona Community (admin. GIA Publications, Inc.). See https://hymnary.org/text/take_this_moment_sign_and_space.

Behold, children are a heritage from the Lord,
the fruit of the womb a reward.
Like arrows in the hand of a warrior
are the children of one's youth.
**Blessed is the man
who fills his quiver with them!
He shall not be put to shame
when he speaks with his enemies in the gate.**

READING (Rom 12:2–21 ESV)

²[Do not be conformed to this world, but be transformed by the renewal of your mind, that by testing you may discern what is the will of God, what is good and acceptable and perfect.]

³For by the grace given to me I say to everyone among you not to think of himself more highly than he ought to think, but to think with sober judgment, each according to the measure of faith that God has assigned. ⁴For as in one body we have many members, and the members do not all have the same function, ⁵so we, though many, are one body in Christ, and individually members one of another. ⁶Having gifts that differ according to the grace given to us, let us use them: if prophecy, in proportion to our faith; ⁷if service, in our serving; the one who teaches, in his teaching; ⁸the one who exhorts, in his exhortation; the one who contributes, in generosity; the one who leads, with zeal; the one who does acts of mercy, with cheerfulness.

⁹[Let love be genuine. Abhor what is evil; hold fast to what is good. ¹⁰Love one another with brotherly affection. Outdo one another in showing honor. ¹¹Do not be slothful in zeal, be fervent in spirit, serve the Lord. ¹²Rejoice in hope, be patient in tribulation, be constant in prayer. ¹³Contribute to the needs of the saints and seek to show hospitality.]

¹⁴Bless those who persecute you; bless and do not curse them. ¹⁵Rejoice with those who rejoice, weep with those who weep. ¹⁶Live in harmony with one another. Do not be haughty, but associate with the lowly. Never be wise in your own sight. ¹⁷Repay no one evil for

evil, but give thought to do what is honorable in the sight of all. [18]If possible, so far as it depends on you, live peaceably with all. [19]Beloved, never avenge yourselves, but leave it to the wrath of God, for it is written, "Vengeance is mine, I will repay, says the Lord." [20]To the contrary, "if your enemy is hungry, feed him; if he is thirsty, give him something to drink; for by so doing you will heap burning coals on his head." [21]Do not be overcome by evil, but overcome evil with good.

REFLECTION

A short reflection may be offered highlighting the stories and experiences of the travelers. The reflection may also suggest calls to action and follow-up work to happen as a result of the pilgrimage.

The reflection should acknowledge the shared community between those who stayed behind, those who traveled, and those met along the way.

PRAYER FOR A NEW TOMORROW

Creating and renewing God,
our journey is not over.
Rather, it is just beginning.
Guide us as we transfer mountaintop experiences
into real action
focused on the kingdom work you would have us do.
May the stories of our travels
meld into the shared story of this faith community.
Renew us, reform us, and refine us
into more faithful disciples
for the new tomorrow you are already preparing for us.
We ask all of this in the name of the triune God:
Creator, Redeemer, and Sustainer.
Amen.

HYMN/SONG *(to be selected from the following)*

"There's a Spirit in the Air"—**LAUDS**[78]
"Now Thank We All Our God"—**NUN DANKET ALLE GOTT**[79]
"We Are Your People"—**WHITFIELD**[80]
"In the Midst of New Dimensions"—**NEW DIMENSIONS**[81]

CLOSING SENTENCES

May the God of hope fill us with all joy and peace (Rom 15:13) through the power of the Holy Spirit.
Amen.

Bless the Lord.
The Lord's name be praised.

DISMISSAL SONG(S)

"Enviado Soy de Dios (The Lord Now Sends Us Forth)"—**ENVIADO**[82]
"Blest Be the Tie That Binds"—**DENNIS**[83]
Additional hymn/song options

    78. Text by Brian A. Wren © 1979 Hope Publishing Company. See https://hymnary.org/text/theres_a_spirit_in_the_air.

    79. Text: Martin Rinkart, c. 1636, translated by Catherine Winkworth, 1858; Music: Johann Crüger, 1647, Public Domain. See https://hymnary.org/text/now_thank_we_all_our_god.

    80. Text by Brian A. Wren © 1975 Hope Publishing Company. See https://hymnary.org/text/we_are_your_people_lord_by_your_grace.

    81. Text and Music by Julian B. Rush © 1994. See https://hymnary.org/text/in_the_midst_of_new_dimensions.

    82. Text: José Aguiar, 20th Century translated by Gerhard M. Cartford, 1998; Music: Pedro Infante, 20th Century, arranged by *Evangelical Lutheran Worship*, 2006; English Translation © 1998 Augsburg Fortress; Music Arrangement © 2003 Augsburg Fortress. See https://hymnary.org/text/the_lord_now_sends_us_forth_with_hands.

    83. Text: John Fawcett, 1782; Music: Johann Georg Nägeli, 1828, arr. Lowell Mason, 1845, Public Domain. See https://hymnary.org/text/blest_be_the_tie_that_binds.

"God, Whose Giving Knows No Ending"—**BEACH SPRING**[84]
"Pues Si Vivimos (When We Are Living)"—**SOMOS DEL SEÑOR**[85]
"Rise, O Church, Like Christ Arisen"—**SURGE ECCLESIA**[86]

Additional musical considerations:
Pilgrimage leaders may also want to substitute hymns throughout these liturgies with secular music and/or songs specifically meaningful to the pilgrimage group. Numerous secular songs from groups like the Beatles, U2, the Eagles, John Denver, Mumford and Sons, etc. may provide significant connection for those traveling. Just as leaders are encouraged to explore worship resources unfamiliar to them as a part of a pilgrimage undertaking, musical resources that connect each individual pilgrim's sense of self should be considered worthy and important parts of the community building process for the group.

---

84. Text: Robert L. Edwards, 1961 © 1961, ren. 1989 *The Hymn Society* (admin. Hope Publishing Company); Music: *The Sacred Harp*, harm. James H. Wood © 1958, ren. 1986 Broadman Press (admin. Music Services). See https://hymnary.org/text/god_whose_giving_knows_no_ending.

85. Text: Stanza 1, anonymous; translated by Elise S. Eslinger, 1983; stanzas 2–4, Roberto Escamilla, 1984 translated by George Lockwood, 1987.
Music: Spanish melody, arr. Barbara C. Mink, 1988.
English Translation © 1989 The United Methodist Publishing House (admin. The Copyright Company).
Spanish Texts Stanzas 2–4 © 1983 Abingdon Press (admin. The Copyright Company). See https://hymnary.org/text/when_we_are_living_it_is_in_christ_jesus.
Music Arrangement © 1988 Barbara C. Mink (admin. Community of Christ).

86. Text: © 1997 Susan Palo Cherwien (admin. Augsburg Fortress); Music: Timothy J. Strand © 1997 Augsburg Fortress. See https://hymnary.org/text/rise_o_church_like_christ_arisen.

From *Plague to Purpose*

QUESTIONNAIRES FOR PILGRIMAGE

For Potential Travelers

This questionnaire is designed to encourage dialogue with potential travelers to ascertain their readiness and understanding of the pilgrimage discipline prior to travel. As discussed in previous chapters, pilgrimage is distinctly different than sacred tourism. Care should be taken to engage potential participants in a discussion of the discipline before departure.

1. Briefly discuss your past travel experiences. How did you encounter God during those journeys—hiking, at meals with fellow pilgrims, at historical sites, in places or at times of worship (gathered or private), in reflections on Scripture, in theological or devotional reading, in singing, etc.?
2. Describe a time where you encountered a different culture or practice from your own background. How did this encounter change your perspective for better or worse?
3. How do you hope this experience will transform your life? Your faith relationship with God? Your wider community and your relationship with others?
4. Describe how you deal with interpersonal conflicts? Pilgrimage often necessitates new relationships with new people and in circumstances and situations different than everyday life. How will you deal with interpersonal conflicts in these situations?
5. What expectations do you have of your traveling companions? Of those charged with your care, shelter, and food during this experience? How do you think those might change as you continue farther along the journey?
6. Describe your own sense of flexibility when pilgrimage necessitates a change in plans, alteration of the schedule, or demands more time.
7. Discuss one intentional practice you would undertake while on pilgrimage?

8. Would you commit to sharing your experiences on pilgrimage with the wider faith community upon return, recognizing that the return is an equal part of the pilgrimage discipline?
9. Finally, briefly describe your reasons for engaging in pilgrimage and your hoped-for conclusions as a result of this journey. What anxieties do you have about this pilgrimage?
10. What are two key words or phrases that summarize your feelings as you begin this pilgrimage? (e.g. adventure, nervous, dread, apprehensive, worried, afraid to let go, etc.)

For Those Remaining at Home

This questionnaire is designed to engage those remaining at home in the pilgrimage discipline so as to prepare them for the hoped-for impact of the pilgrimage discipline on the wider faith community. It is also meant to encourage solidarity with those traveling throughout the duration of the trip.

1. Briefly discuss your perceptions of how the stories of those returning from pilgrimage may impact the wider faith community.
2. How might you support the pilgrimage community at the different stages of their journey—before departing, while they travel, and upon their return?
3. Will you be open to the stories, insights, and wisdom gained by these travelers when they return home?
4. What expectations do you have for these travelers as it relates to the wider faith community when they return?
5. How will you deal with revelations, stories, practices, or experiences shared by these travelers that differ from the normal experiences of the faith community? Do these things have a place in the postpilgrimage life of the community?
6. What intentional practice would you consider undertaking in solidarity with these travelers while they are gone?
7. Briefly describe your understandings of pilgrimage and the reasons for the faith community to support such endeavors.

For the Return

This questionnaire is designed to be completed by travelers upon completion of the pilgrimage journey.

1. Describe your experience of the pilgrimage. Where/when did you experience the closest relationship with God? With the community of pilgrims?
2. What was the highlight of the experience for you?
3. What were the most difficult parts of the pilgrimage? How did you deal with them?
4. How has engagement with the pilgrimage discipline renewed, strengthened, or transformed your faith? Or not?
5. Were any experiences, people, or practices surprising? How will these experiences shape your expectations of faith practices, relationship, etc. in the future?
6. Is there a passage of Scripture or a song (or both) that has become particularly meaningful or which summarizes the pilgrimage for you? Why?
7. Do you feel called to action as a result of pilgrimage? If so, in what ways?
8. What would you have the wider faith community know and understand as a result of this journey?

AN ANNOTATED LIST OF POTENTIAL PILGRIMAGE SITES

Each individual or group must discern what site (if any) of pilgrimage makes the most sense for their purposes. As discussed in previous chapters, a wider definition of pilgrimage allows for any site to become a place of sacred journeying. Additionally, pilgrimage may be metaphorical, with an individual or group engaging in its practices without leaving home. The list below suggests some potential sites and reasons for their consideration.

Holy Land (Israel/Palestine)

The modern understanding of pilgrimage began with trips to the Holy Land. Selecting Israel/Palestine as a site of pilgrimage offers the opportunity to engage with the sites (or believed sites) of the biblical narrative. However, a postmodern approach to a pilgrimage in Israel/Palestine might focus on exploring the intersection of diverse cultures and taking a critical look at religious tolerance/intolerance and its connection with global justice and peace. Jerusalem, in particular, also provides a distinctive musical soundscape as a part of the pilgrimage discipline.[87] The sounds, music, and sung prayers of Jewish, Islamic, and Christian pilgrims converge in very close proximity to one another, creating the potential for a broader dialogue about the pilgrimage group's relationship with other cultures and worldviews.

Rome/Vatican City (Italy)

Similar to Israel/Palestine, a pilgrimage to Rome is imbued with historical connections to the Christian faith and the pilgrimage discipline. However, as the center of the Roman Catholic Church, Rome/Vatican City stand at the epicenter of a church largely in decline in the northern hemisphere, and one rife with scandal. A postmodern approach to pilgrimage in Rome/Vatican City may focus on the need to reform the church in the twenty-first century. Additionally, the art and architecture of the city may provide for a completely different experience of pilgrimage focused on creative expressions of faith.

The Island of Iona/The Iona Community (Scotland)

A pilgrimage to the isle of Iona in Scotland is multifaceted. A journey to Iona presents varied, often challenging transportation issues that may become a pilgrimage in their own right. After arriving on Iona, participants in a program week of the Iona Community will

---

87. Wood, "Soundscapes of Pilgrimage," 286.

experience a pilgrimage guided by the daily routine and activities of the community. However, the island also provides an ecumenical history and story of its own. At the heart of the Iona experience is a focus on community—whether experienced through the work of the Iona Community or as a guest in one of the island's hotels. A postmodern approach to a pilgrimage on Iona might consider new forms of community, interconnectedness, and renewal. Additionally, for the Iona Community, a great focus on justice and peace when pilgrims return to their own communities is of the utmost importance. See chapter 4 for additional information.

Pilgrimage to Other Islands

Other islands may also provide unique opportunities for pilgrimage due to their limited scope, remoteness, and potential for in-depth exploration. Some islands to consider might include the Galápagos Islands in Ecuador, Easter Island in Chile, Lindisfarne in England, among others.

The Taizé Community (France)

The Taizé Community offers week-long programs for those who join in the daily life of the community. According to their website, "a stay in Taizé can help one step back from daily life, to meet a wide variety of people and consider one's commitment in the Church and in society."[88] Focused on providing space for reconciliation, a postmodern pilgrimage today provides the opportunity to consider how personal discipleship relates to the challenges of society.

Camino de Santiago de Compostela (Spain)

"The Way of St. James" is an ancient pilgrimage route. Perhaps the best walking pilgrimage of the historic sites, the *camino* offers an opportunity to engage in the journey in a different way than the

88. "Coming to Taizé," para. 2.

other sites. A postmodern approach to this pilgrimage may focus on the shared human experience and the various reasons individuals choose to undertake pilgrimage.

Assisi, Italy

The center of St. Francis of Assisi's ministry, this town in Italy is a popular pilgrimage destination for walking pilgrimages similar to the Camino de Santiago de Compostela focused on the life and teachings of Francis. A postmodern approach to this pilgrimage may focus on the stewardship of creation and ecumenicism.

Pilgrimage to Other Monastic Communities

Other monastic communities offer short-term pilgrimage opportunities to visit and join in the communal life of their order. Sites such as the Christ in the Desert Monastery[89] or various Chemin neuf Communities (https://us.chemin-neuf.org/) provide pilgrimage opportunities in various locations that allow pilgrims to engage in countercultural practices and communal living.

Washington DC

Not a religious site of pilgrimage, Washington DC provides American pilgrims with an experience to explore the intersection of national identity and faith. Venues such as the National Museum of African American History, the National Gallery of Art, and the National Museum of the American Indian may provide opportunities for pilgrims to explore the connection between faith, the church, and stewardship of creation, human rights, and justice issues. Additionally, the pilgrimage may focus on the political nature of the gospel and the real-world implications of discipleship.

---

89. https://christdesert.org/.

Pilgrimage in Nature

Nature walks or travel to remote places may serve as a site of pilgrimage focused on God's creation, stewardship of creation, and the relationship between humanity and the earth. Special care should be given to ways to build community among pilgrims while lessening the impact of their presence on the environment.

Pilgrimage to an Art Museum

Similar to the art and architecture of Rome, more local museums and sites may also become the sites of pilgrimage stressing the connection between the pilgrimage discipline and the impact upon the larger faith community. Leaders should consider practices that can make a visit to these sites more than just a sight-seeing trip.

Pilgrimage in the Local Community

The ways in which the life of the faith community shapes and is shaped by the local municipality may yield a different kind of pilgrimage experience. Through commitment to visiting local sites, studying local history, and sharing prayer related to the community, a pilgrimage group may find that it is not necessary to travel to engage the pilgrimage discipline. How these experiences are shared with the larger faith community may also result in a renewed energy for the ministry and mission of the congregation.

Pilgrimage with the Poor

Modeled after the Taizé brothers' ministry in Hell's Kitchen in New York, or Mother Teresa's work in India, pilgrimage groups may be able to design a pilgrimage experience that encourages solidarity with the poor in their own community. This would not be a short-term mission project but rather a way of praying and joining in life with this community.

Pilgrimage to Nowhere

Finally, it may be possible for a group of pilgrims to engage in practices together that do not require travel. Through intentional practice, community-building, seeking transformation through group interaction, a metaphorical pilgrimage may be possible. Christine Valters Painter's book, *The Soul of a Pilgrim,* and other similar resources may be used in a class setting to study and engage with pilgrimage ideas without leaving home.

6

Coda

THE SHAPE OF PILGRIMAGE

Biblical narratives and historical accounts make a compelling case for the rediscovery of pilgrimage in the twenty-first century. The Christian faith is rooted in the balance between individual discipleship and communal experience. Pilgrimage, defined by individual constructs of meaning and carried out in groups—either intentionally formed or formed along the journey—offers an important means for achieving this balance with potential ramifications for the postmodern church (see chapter 1 for a fuller discussion of pilgrimage's benefits for the postmodern church). As Joerg Rieger puts it, "Christianity comes alive only on the road."[1] Of course, traveling or sacred journeying may mean different things to different people. In the process of seeking the divine through pilgrimage, one size does not fit all. As demonstrated, the practices of pilgrimage—prayer, worship, and music among others—potentially shape the meaning of any pilgrimage experience as much as the destination itself.

---

1. Rieger, *Faith on the Road*, 39.

Coda

The practices of pilgrimage invite individuals to construct meaning on their own terms, and the communal negotiation of that which is best for the entire group creates a powerful connection, or *communitas,* and liminal moments among the pilgrimage travelers. This connection to one another allows the group to approach their destination from a place of vulnerability, an aspect of liminality that hopefully facilitates transformation. The labyrinth of the pilgrimage discipline must include these steps and practices, not simply arrival at a location, in order to distinguish it from sacred tourism. It is the practices and community building aspects of the discipline that signify something is different; potentially reshaping the pilgrim's expectations both on the journey and in their return to the local faith community.[2]

While modern forms of travel may not create the same hardship that medieval-era pilgrims endured while journeying, pilgrimage in the twenty-first century must reach beyond simple expectations that things will be easy, remain the same, or conform to the American Christian ethos. A rediscovery of the ways in which the sacred adjusts to the concerns of pilgrims rather than the concerns of the pilgrims reshaping the sacred is essential to the success of any pilgrimage undertaking. It is this readjustment that may lead to a reexamination of the established church's story upon the pilgrim's return.[3]

Any reexamination of one's story, or a faith community's story, does not come without challenge. However, the moments of encounter with other people, music, worship, and other practices on pilgrimage provide a platform for this discernment connected to rich experiences. These encounters compel all involved, both those traveling and those who remain at home, to question their own assertions and ways of being. The attention to intention on pilgrimage produces opportunities to broaden one's horizons and open one's self to a new experience of the divine in ways antithetical to many other traditions in the current church.

---

2. Rieger, *Faith on the Road,* 66.
3. Rieger, *Faith on the Road,* 66.

From *Plague* to *Purpose*

ATTENTION TO INTENTION

Travel may make a difference in the discussion of the postmodern church's relevancy. Pilgrimage may produce conversations around the church's purpose and a hoped-for transformation, with a commitment to the valuing and incorporation of insights gained on the journey into the faith community's life together. As Phil Cousineau states, "There is no such thing as a neutral act, an empty thought, an aimless day. Travels become sacred by the depths of their contemplations."[4] How an individual or community incorporates and reflects upon the practices of prayer, musicmaking, journaling, and daily worship experienced *on* pilgrimage in their lives *post-pilgrimage* will ultimately determine the success or impact of the discipline in the long term.

The long-term impacts of the discipline stand in contrast to the often misdirected focus of short-term mission trips. Pilgrimage is about transformation of self and community through encounter rather than a prideful conclusion focused on the community's perceived ability to help.[5] The hoped-for transformation of pilgrimage roots itself not in short-term gains but in a deeper understanding of everyday life, faith, and community. For the disciples, following Jesus meant giving up every aspect of their lives. The cycle of pilgrimage includes a return, but it likely necessitates the giving up of life as it was known.

TRANSFORMATION

Ultimately, pilgrimage is rooted in tension, displacement, and the cycle of disorientation and reorientation. New understandings are gained through encounters with God along the journey. These transformations often require ceding control and developing a more flexible approach, focused on the movement of the Holy Spirit, rather than the maintenance of the status quo. The pilgrimage discipline overturns preconceived notions, leading to the

---

4. Cousineau, *Art of Pilgrimage*, 106.
5. Rieger, *Faith on the Road*, 53.

transformation of self for the individual and, potentially, for the reformation of entire communities and systems. Music is one connectional tool for this process.

Singing the song of the other highlights the broader horizons to which pilgrimage beckons. This music, along with exposure to diverse worship practices, prayer, and encounters with people from differing backgrounds, traditions, and cultures, presents important transformative moments not only for the individual traveler but for the church and the world. This positions pilgrimage, with its music and other practices, as a significant resource for the evolving, reforming life of the Christian church today.

Bibliography

Balado, José Luis González. *The Story of Taizé*. New York: Seabury, 1981.
Bauman, Zygmunt. "From Pilgrim to Tourist—Or a Short History of Identity." In *Questions of Cultural Identity*, edited by Stuart and Paul du Gay Hall, 18–36. London: SAGE, 1996.
Bell, John L. *The Truth That Sets Us Free: Biblical Songs for Worship*. Glasgow: Wild Goose, 2012.
———. *We Walk His Way: Shorter Songs for Worship*. Chicago: GIA, 2008.
Bell, John L., and Allison Adam. *Sing the World: Global Songs for Children*. Glasgow: Wild Goose, 2008.
Bentley, Jane. "Community, Authenticity, Growth: The Role of Musical Participation in the Iona Community's Island Centres." *International Journal of Community Music* 2.1 (March 2009) 71–77.
Bethge, Eberhard. *Dietrich Bonhoeffer: Man of Vision, Man of Courage*. New York: Harper, 1970.
Bohlman, Philip V. "The Final Borderpost." *The Journal of Musicology* 14.4 (Fall 1996) 427–52.
———. "Pilgrimage." *Grove Music Online*, January 20. 2001. https://doi.org/10.1093/gmo/9781561592630.article.46448.
———. "Pilgrimage, Politics, and the Musical Remapping of the New Europe." *Ethnomusicology* 40.3 (Fall 1996) 375–412.
Book of Common Worship. Louisville: Westminster John Knox, 2018.
Bradley, Ian. *Columba: Pilgrim and Penitent*. Glasgow: Wild Goose, 1996.
Brueggemann, Walter. *The Land: Place as Gift, Promise, and Challenge in Biblical Faith*. Philadelphia: Fortress, 1977.
Bunyan, John. *The Pilgrim's Progress*. London: The Religious Tract Society, 1851.
Campbell, Joseph. *The Hero with a Thousand Faces*. New York: Meridian, 1968.
Chaucer, Geoffrey. *Canterbury Tales*. Edited by Geraldine McCaughrean. London: Penguin, 2015.
Church Hymnary IV: Words. Norwich, UK: Canterbury, 2007.
Collins-Kreiner, Noga. "Researching Pilgrimage: Continuity and Transformations." *Annals of Tourism Research* 37.2 (April 2010) 440–56.

Bibliography

"Coming to Taizé." https://www.taize.fr/en_rubrique9.html.

Cousineau, Phil. *The Art of Pilgrimage: The Seeker's Guide to Making Travel Sacred.* San Francisco: Conari, 1998.

Cousins, Melinda. "Conversing with the God of the Pilgrimage Psalms." *St Mark's Review* 239 (March 2017) 35–50.

Curran, Ian. "Theology as Spiritual Discipline." *Liturgy* 26.1 (November 2010) 3–10.

Eliot, T. S. *Four Quartets.* London: Faber & Faber, 2019.

Evangelical Lutheran Worship. Minneapolis: Augsburg Fortress, 2016.

Ferguson, Ronald. *Chasing the Wild Goose: The Story of the Iona Community.* Glasgow: Wild Goose, 1998.

Frank, Georgia. "Pilgrimage." In *The Oxford Handbook of Early Christian Studies*, edited by Susan Ashbrook Harvey and David G. Hunter, 826–42. Oxford: Oxford University Press, 2008.

Gennep, Arnold van, et al. *The Rites of Passage.* Chicago: University of Chicago Press, 1960.

George, Christian. *Sacred Travels: Recovering the Ancient Practice of Pilgrimage.* Downers Grove, IL: InterVarsity, 2006.

Gregory of Nyssa. *On the Soul and the Resurrection.* Translated by Catharine P. Roth. Crestwood, NY: St. Vladimir's Seminary Press, 1993.

Hawn, C. Michael. *Gather into One: Praying and Singing Globally.* Grand Rapids: Eerdmans, 2003.

———. *New Songs of Celebration Render: Congregational Song in the Twenty-First Century.* Chicago: GIA, 2013.

Hornabrook, Jasmine. "Songs of the Saints: Song Paths and Pilgrimage in London's Tamil Hindu Diaspora." *Asian Music* 49.2 (Summer 2018) 106–50.

Ingalls, Monique. "Singing Heaven Down to Earth: Spiritual Journeys, Eschatological Sounds, and Community Formation in Evangelical Conference Worship." *Ethnomusicology* 55.2 (Spring/Summer 2011) 255–79.

Iona Abbey Worship Book. Glasgow: Wild Goose, 2001.

Kubicki, Judith M. *Liturgical Music as Ritual Symbol: A Case Study of Jacques Berthier's Taizé Music.* Leuven: Peeters, 1999.

———. 2013. "Taizé (USA)." *Grove Music Online.* http://www.oxfordmusiconline.com/subscriber/article/grove/music/A2252419.

Lang, Paul H. *The Pilgrim's Compass: Finding and Following the God We Seek.* Louisville: Westminster John Knox, 2019.

Lipka, Michael, and Claire Gecewicz. "More Americans Now Say They're Spiritual But Not Religious." *Pew Research Center*, September 6, 2017. https://www.pewresearch.org/fact-tank/2017/09/06/more-americans-now-say-theyre-spiritual-but-not-religious/.

MacCannell, Dean. *Empty Meeting Grounds.* New York: Routledge, 1992.

Niebuhr, Richard R. "Pilgrims and Pioneers." *Parabola* 9.3 (1984) 7.

Opstal, Sandra Maria van. *The Next Worship: Glorifying God in a Diverse World.* Downers Grove, IL: InterVarsity, 2016.

BIBLIOGRAPHY

Painter, Christine Valters. *The Soul of a Pilgrim: Eight Practices for the Journey Within.* Notre Dame: Sorin, 2015.

Pazos, Antón M. *Pilgrims and Politics: Rediscovering the Power of the Pilgrimage.* New York: Ashgate, 2012.

Pew Research Center. "Global Christianity—A Report on the Size and Distribution of the World's Christian Population." December 19, 2011. https://www.pewresearch.org/religion/2011/12/19/global-christianity-exec/.

Pilgrim, Peace. *Peace Pilgrim: Her Life and Work in Her Own Words.* Shelton, CT: Friends of Peace Pilgrim/Ocean Tree, 2013.

Power, Rosemary. "A Place of Community: 'Celtic' Iona and Institutional Religion." *Folklore* 117.1 (April 2006) 33–53.

Reily, Suzel Ana. *Voices of the Magi: Enchanted Journeys in Southeast Brazil.* Chicago: University of Chicago Press, 2002.

Rieger, Joerg. *Faith on the Road: A Short Theology of Travel and Justice.* Downers Grove, IL: InterVarsity, 2015.

Robinson, Martin. *Sacred Places, Pilgrim Paths: An Anthology of Pilgrimage.* London: Harper Collins, 1997.

Ruf, Frederick J. *Bewildered Travel: The Sacred Quest for Confusion.* Charlottesville: University of Virginia Press, 2007.

Russell, Letty M. *Church in the Round: Feminist Interpretation of the Church.* Louisville: Westminster John Knox, 1993.

Sallnow, M. J. "Communitas Reconsidered: The Sociology of Andean Pilgrimage." *Man* 16.2 (June 1981) 163–82.

Santos, Jason Brian. *A Community Called Taizé: A Story of Prayer, Worship, and Reconciliation.* Downers Grove, IL: InterVarsity, 2008.

Sargeant, Wendi, *Christian Education and the Emerging Church: Postmodern Faith Formation.* Eugene, OR: Pickwick, 2015.

Socolov, Emily. "Pilgrimage." *Folklore* 3 (2011) 995–98.

Stokes, Martin. "Travel and Tourism: An Afterword." *The World of Music* 41.3 (1999) 141–55.

Thomas, Simon, et al. "To Pray and to Play: Post-Postmodern Pilgrimage at Lourdes." *Tourism Management* 68 (October 2018) 412–22.

Tice, Adam M. L. *Stars Like Grace: 50 More Hymn Texts.* Chicago: GIA, 2013.

Tolan, John Victor. *Saint Francis and the Sultan: The Curious History of a Christian-Muslim Encounter.* Oxford: Oxford University Press, 2009.

Turner, Victor. "Passages, Margins, and Poverty: Religious Symbols of Communitas." *Worship* 46 (October 1972) 390–412.

———. "Process, System, and Symbol: A New Anthropological Synthesis." *Daedalus* 106.3 (Summer 1977) 61–80.

———. *The Ritual Process: Structure and Anti-Structure.* Chicago: Aldine, 1969.

Turner, Victor W., and Edith L. B. Turner. *Image and Pilgrimage in Christian Culture: Anthropological Perspectives.* New York: Columbia University Press, 1978.

Twain, Mark. *The Innocents Abroad.* New York: Chelsea House, 2021.

BIBLIOGRAPHY

The United Methodist Book of Worship. Nashville: United Methodist Publishing House, 2009.

Witvliet, John D., et al. *Psalms for All Seasons: A Complete Psalter for Worship*. Grand Rapids: Calvin Institute of Christian Worship, 2012.

Wood, Abigail. "Soundscapes of Pilgrimage: European and American Christians in Jerusalem's Old City." *Ethnomusicology Forum* 23.3 (December 2014) 285–305.

www.ingramcontent.com/pod-product-compliance
Lightning Source LLC
Chambersburg PA
CBHW072148160426
43197CB00012B/2299